UNDER HIS WINGS
The Gospel According to Ruth

Rich Lusk
and Uri Brito

ATHANASIUS
PRESS
WEST MONROE, LOUISIANA

Under His Wings: The Gospel According to Ruth
Copyright © 2018 by Athanasius Press
715 Cypress Street
West Monroe, Louisiana 71291
www.athanasiuspress.org

ISBN: 978-0-615-90938-7 (softcover)

Contents

ACKNOWLEDGEMENTS

This project began six years ago with a transcript from Pastor Lusk's Sunday School studies on Ruth. Our thanks to Cathy Honeycutt who transcribed those audio lectures. Were it not for her efforts it's likely this commentary would not exist. Those early transcriptions provided the foundation for the body of this work.

We also cannot even begin to express our gratitude to James B. Jordan whose exegetical genius in his lectures on Ruth inspired us in preparing this commentary. Jim's influence is seen throughout and we rightly honor his faithful labors.

We wish to thank the many gifted friends who looked over early drafts and offered fruitful insights, especially Heather Johnson, Rob Hadding, Dustin Messer, and Ron Gilley.

Finally, our thanks to Athanasius Press who saw the potential for such a project and encouraged us to persevere.

PREFACE TO THE READER

The reader should know a few things about this book before beginning. First, both authors would like to thank James B. Jordan for his pioneering work in the Old Testament, including the book of Ruth. His fingerprints are all over this mini-commentary. We take full responsibility for the work, but Jordan deserves a lot of credit for anything we get right.

Second, this commentary is not intended to be a rigorously academic work. We do expect it to withstand scholarly scrutiny, but it also takes many things for granted that are argued for elsewhere. In particular, the biblical and canonical theology of James B. Jordan is critical to this work. Those who want to pursue further the issues of canonical placement and typology in Ruth should consult Jordan's various works, especially his lectures on wordmp3.com.

Third, this commentary was produced from transcripts of Sunday School lessons taught by Pastor Lusk in 2004. While we have cleaned up a good bit of the language and made it slightly more formal, it is always challenging to transform the spoken word into the written word. Stylistically, we have not always tried to hide the fact that this work grew out of Sunday School classes that were quite informal and conversational. That also accounts for some occasional repetition.

Finally, we hope to produce a commentary on Ruth that, while not dealing exhaustively with the text in all its dimensions, will give the reader a firm grasp of the "gospel according to Ruth." We hope that pastors and teachers who are preaching and teaching through Ruth will find this work useful, but we also hope it will be helpful to faithful believers looking for ways to encounter Scripture in a way that is richly devotional yet also theologically deep. All too often devotional readings lack theological and exegetical content, while exegetical and theological works lack practical devotion. We hope this short work can help bridge this unfortunate gap.

Uri Brito

THE LITTLEST GOSPEL: INTRODUCING RUTH

Ruth is a carefully crafted story. Every reader agrees it is a wonderful little narrative. Some commentators have even called it a "novella," a short novel. Some have classified its genre as "short story" or "folk tale."

These kinds of labels are fine as long as we maintain the historicity of the book. All of the internal evidence in this book indicates that it is written as a *true* story. It is not presented merely as a charming little folk narrative or a romantic fantasy, but as redemptive history. C.S. Lewis and J.R.R. Tolkien spoke of the gospel as the "true myth."[1] We might think of Ruth as the "true novel" or the "true romance."

---

1   C.S. Lewis, "Myth Became Fact," in *God in the Dock: Essays on Theology and Ethics*, ed. by Walter Hooper (Grand Rapids, MI: Wm B. Eerdmans Publishing Co., 1944; reprint, 2001), 63-67.

"...but Christians also need to be reminded . . . that what became Fact was a Myth, that it carries with it into the world of Fact all the properties of a myth. God is more than a god, not less; Christ is more than Balder, not less. We must not be ashamed of the mythical radiance resting on our theology....We must not, in false spirituality, withhold our imaginative welcome. If God chooses to be mythopoeic....shall we refuse to be mythopathic? For this is the marriage of heaven and earth: Perfect Myth and Perfect Fact: claiming not only our love and

The Bible is a storybook. It gives us one over-arching story of God and his creation. From Genesis to Revelation, Scripture provides us with a narrative that encompasses creation, fall, and re-creation. It is a story that runs the whole course of human history, from the first things to the last things. But within the Bible's big story, there are several little stories that reflect the whole story, which gives us the Bible in a nutshell. These micro-narratives crystallize the biblical meta-narrative.

Ruth is one of those micro-narratives. In just over 80 verses, God's whole redemptive program for creation is summarized and enacted in miniature. This story, in other words, gives us the gospel in the form of a short story. Ruth is a lens through which we can see the entirety of redemptive history. Of course, "The Gospel According to Ruth" is the same gospel found everywhere else in Scripture. Ruth is typological drama as well as a Christocentric, prophetic narrative that shows us how God will rescue his people. It may be a romantic story, but it is fundamentally a *theological romance*, for it points beyond the love that Ruth and Boaz have for one another to the love affair between Christ and his church. This story's meaning lies at the heart of history, namely, God's redeeming love for his bride.

The Authorship of Ruth

Before we can get into looking at how the book of Ruth works as a gospel story, we need to consider a few background items. We start with the question of authorship. Who wrote the book of Ruth? We know the book is divinely inspired, but can we pin down the Spirit's human agent? Ruth comes to us anonymously, and identifying the author with confidence is not an easy task. One commentator describes it as "an exercise in futility."[2] But biblical

---

our obedience, but also our wonder and delight...."

2   Frederic W. Bush, *Ruth/Esther*, World Biblical Commentary Book 9 (Dallas, Texas: Thomas Nelson Inc., 1996), 514.

scholars are rarely content to let such questions go unanswered, so several candidates have been identified. Samuel and Solomon are the most popular guesses.

The rabbinic tradition, including the Talmud, attributes the book to Samuel. We know Samuel from the book that bears his name. He was the child of Hannah, raised at the temple, and called to be the Lord's prophet. He anointed Saul as Israel's king and later anointed David as king. Samuel would undoubtedly have a reason for writing; he needed to show why David was a legitimate choice to supplant Saul. If the transition from the house of Saul (and the possible dynasty that ultimately failed because of Saul's sin) to the house of David (an unknown, not even respected in his own family during his youth) is to be made smoothly, a defense of David's background is necessary. Ruth was written, at least in part, to satisfy this purpose — to show why David has a legitimate right to bear office in Israel, despite coming from Judah's bastard line and a Moabite ancestress.

Some of the evidence for authorship could certainly apply to Samuel, but there a few problems with suggesting he is the author. Most of the objections to his authorship have to do with timing. Most significantly, the concluding genealogy of the book of Ruth presupposes that David is a well-known figure and, in fact, seems to assume that he has already become king in an official and open sense. For example, Samuel anoints David as king in 1 Samuel 16, but David doesn't become king over Israel until much later — indeed, not until after Samuel's death.

There is also the matter of the custom explained in Ruth 4:7: to seal the deal between Boaz and the unnamed kinsman of Naomi. The fact that the ritual required an explanation in the text could indicate the book was written much later, as though the custom had fallen out of use by the time of composition.

All these objections can be overcome. They may wound the idea that Samuel was the author, but none of them kills it altogether. For example, Samuel's anointing of David, as well as his knowledge that David would one day rise to kingly fame, may have justified writing the genealogy as he did. Moreover, it is not as though David was a completely unknown figure after 1 Samuel 16.

Further, the explanation of the custom in Ruth 4:7 could have been added in later by an inspired editor. There are many places in Scripture where a later generation of inspired editors slightly altered a canonical text. For example, in Genesis 14, we find some explanatory comments about details that were likely not included in the original Genesis text. The additional comments in Genesis 14 were later added by another inspired writer to make correlations with other Biblical texts or to allow a later audience to understand more clearly what was going on. The record of Moses' death at the end of Deuteronomy is another possible example of inspired edits. It is possible such edits were made to the book of Ruth, though it is difficult to say for sure.

If Ruth was written after the time of Judges, then Solomon becomes a viable candidate for author. Solomon could have penned Ruth with a view to justifying his father's kingship against various challenges and, of course, by implication, defending his own kingship. Note that Solomon oversaw the construction of the temple, and one of the great pillars in the temple that Solomon built is named Boaz. It is possible Solomon wrote this book to show why one of the pillars in the temple was named after his ancestor. In fact, in some versions of the Hebrew canon, the book of Ruth is grouped with several of Solomon's writings, particularly with Song of Solomon and Ecclesiastes.

A third but less popular possibility is David himself. Again, David would be writing to justify his kingship and the transition from the house of Saul to his own house. In fact, if David was the author, it is possible he wrote the book as sort of an instruction manual for his son, Solomon, as if to say, "Son, look at Boaz. This is is the kind of man Israel needs. You see what Boaz did for Ruth and Naomi. Israel needs a king who will care for the nation in the same way. Israel needs a king like Boaz. Be that kind of king." Davidic authorship becomes unlikely when one looks at the book's end. The last word in the book of Ruth is the name of

David. It would be uncharacteristic for David as the author to end the book with his own name. Perhaps it could have been done with appropriate humility, but it seems unlikely.

In the end, we have to admit we do not know the identity of the human author with certainty. What is most important for us to remember is that behind the human author, whoever he was, stands the divine author. Ruth is God's story; it is God's word to us, for our good.

THE CIRCUMSTANCES AND DATING OF RUTH

When dating the book of Ruth, we run into some of the same kind of ambiguities as authorship. First, we must determine when the story took place. Ruth is set during a famine in the period of the judges, which stretches from roughly 1400 B.C. to about 1050 B.C. Certain segments of time within the period of the judges can be ruled out. For example, Judges 3 describes a period when the Moabites oppressed Israel. Given that Elimelech takes his family over into the region of Moab, it seems implausible that the story took place during the time frame of Judges 3, during which the Moabites were persecuting and harassing Israel.

Given the circumstantial evidence, the story is likely set in the time of the Midianite invasions described in Judges 6. The Midianites were agents of God's chastisement, oppressing Israel because of her sin until Gideon finally drove them out. The Midianites would come in, particularly during harvest season, to raid and destroy Israel's crops and steal Israel's harvest. That little detail in the book of Judges possibly explains how there could be a famine in Bethlehem, yet not in nearby Moab. The famine in Bethlehem might have been due to Midianite invasion, rather than natural causes such as weather patterns.

If the story took place concurrent with events described in Judges 6, when was the story written down? Some scholars suggest a very late date, even the post-exilic period, but the reasons given are usually very weak. It makes much better sense to date the book about the time of David's reign since it ends with David as king. Furthermore, Ruth is probably written, to some extent at least, to justify the transfer of power from Saul's house to David's line. Thus, it is probable that the book of Ruth was composed not too long after the events it records took place, most likely during the reign of David or Solomon (roughly 1000 B.C.)

THE PURPOSE OF RUTH

We cannot fully determine Ruth's purpose without having studied the book itself, but we can offer a thumbnail sketch of the book's events. Ruth's placement in the canon tells us something about the book's purpose. We might not be accustomed to attributing any significance to the place of a book in the biblical canon; after all, God has not given us an inspired table of contents that prescribes exactly how the canonical writings are to be organized. But consider the order of the canon as it has come down to us.

First, we have the Pentateuch, the so-called five books of Moses: Genesis, Exodus, Leviticus, Numbers, and Deuteronomy. At least parts of Genesis likely predated Moses, but he appears to be responsible for bringing the five books together into a unit. Then we have Joshua, which is written about the same time, not long after the death of Moses, and which records what happens in the next generation, namely the conquest of the promised land under Joshua, Moses' successor. Then we have Judges, which is the seventh book; Ruth follows as the eighth book. Now, think about those books in the sixth, seventh, and eighth slots. Joshua is the sixth book and includes a lot of references about entering into the land, which is also described as entering into God's rest. The people will enter into a kind of permanent Sabbath rest when they settle in the land. But Joshua is the sixth book, which tells us that this Sabbath rest is not going to be the final Sabbath that God planned for his people; rather, it is only going to be a type or shadow of it. The New Testament book of Hebrews reinforces this point. The people entered into God's rest when they entered into the land, but only in a typological form. Only in the New

Covenant do we move out of the sixth and into the promised seventh, the promised rest of God. So Joshua was only a shadow of the one to come, a greater Joshua, who would bring the people into a greater promised inheritance, and who would provide that promised Sabbath rest by bringing us out of the sixth and into the seventh day (Matt. 11:28-29).

Judges is the seventh book. Now the number seven, of course, is the number of perfection. But the book of Judges is not about perfection at all unless you want to think of it as Israel "perfecting" various ways to rebel against God. The only thing that gets perfected in the book of Judges is Israel's sin of idolatry. But there is an interesting connection here. If one reads Genesis 1-3 as a sequential, historical narrative (as we should), Gen. 1:1-2:4 gives an overall creation account up through the seventh day when God rested. Genesis 2:5ff takes us back to Day Six and puts the creation of man under a microscope. We are now given a lot of details from the sixth day of creation that were omitted in the initial macro-account. Day Six, because of its importance, is singled out in Genesis 2, as everything focuses in on man as the chief and crowning work of God in creation. But if we keep reading (and ignore the chapter breaks, which are added later for convenience), we come to the account of the fall. Genesis 3 seems to detail the occurrences of that first Sabbath day. There are several reasons for viewing Genesis 3 as the first Sabbath. This is the day in which Adam and Eve went into that central sanctuary area of the Garden of Eden to meet with God. In other words, this was clearly the time of special worship, which, in the rest of the Old Covenant, is a seventh-day event. So it makes good sense to see this as the day that the Lord is going to walk in the garden and meet with them. The Sabbath day is the day of meeting between God and his people. Sadly, before the Lord gets there, Adam and Eve jump the gun and steal from the tree of the knowledge of good and evil. They eat the forbidden fruit and, of course, we know what happens from there.

So the seventh day was to be the day of relaxation in God's presence, the day of covenant renewal with God, the day of rejoicing in God's presence, and of receiving gifts from God's hand. But Adam and Eve fell on the seventh day. They committed treason in the sanctuary. In light of this creational pattern, consider Judges, the seventh book of the canon. What correspondences do we see between the first seven books of the canon and the first week of history described in Genesis 1-3? In a sense, you could say the fall is brought to its culmination point in the book of Judges. In the book of Judges, things get as bad as they can possibly get. Judges shows us the fall of Adam and Eve carried out to its most extreme form, as God's people complete their rebellion against him. Remember, this is Israel, the chosen nation of Yahweh, a race of new Adams and new Eves. These are the people who are supposed to serve as the representatives of God to humanity and who are supposed to represent humanity before God. As we read the book of Judges, we find God's people have things completely backward. They are calling white black; they're calling the light darkness. Everything is flip-flopped in the book of Judges. The judges themselves, of course, are faithful (for the most part) and redeem the people. But even then, as soon as they rescue the people, almost invariably within a generation, the people lapse into an idolatry even worse than before. And as we progress through the book, the good times aren't so good anymore, and the bad times get even worse. The priests, who were supposed to lead the people in the knowledge of God, actually lead them into gross idolatry. The book of Judges is a very sad tale; it's a very sad collection of stories about Israel's fallenness.

JUDGES AS THE OLD CREATION

How does the book of Judges end? We get an analysis of Israel's root problem in 21:25: "In those days, there was no king in Israel, everyone did what was right in his own eyes."

This is a dark, dark time in Israel's history, but this evaluation of the problem is highly ironic. Was there a king in Israel during the time of Judges? Yes, of course, there was a king. Yahweh himself was Israel's king. She had everything she needed if she would only submit to Yahweh's reign and lordship over her. But because she continually rejected Yahweh and did not want Yahweh to be king over her, everything in Israel is a disaster. And so what does Yahweh need to do? He needs to set up a human representative of his own kingship over the people. He needs to give to his people a human icon of his lordship to remind them of his character, purposes, and presence.

The book of Judges ends on this very sad note. It ends with this declaration that there is no king in Israel, so everybody is doing what is right in his own eyes. But it is precisely in this period of ethical chaos and theological disorder that God's salvation bursts forth. Out of this dark seventh day comes a ray of shining light, an eighth day, an eighth book. Of course, the number 8 is the number of new creation. The old creation is fallen and falling apart, so we need a new creation. This is why the number 8 is so significant in Scripture. Eight is the number of a new birth, a new week, and a new beginning. Circumcision takes place on the eighth day. The child lives through the old creation week, but because the first creation is fallen, on the eighth day he must be fully incorporated into the new humanity of Israel. The eighth day is the day of the resurrection. It's the first day of a new week when God raises up Jesus. The gospels' resurrection accounts are filled with creation imagery pointing us to the fact that Jesus has, in fact, inaugurated a new world order in his resurrection on the eighth day. For example, at the end of John's gospel when Mary comes to the tomb (which is in a garden.), she sees Jesus, but she mistakes him for the gardener. But this is no mistake at all — he is the new Gardener, the new Adam. Then the risen Lord meets with his disciples on consecutive eighth days. Thomas is not there the first time. Certainly, Jesus could have appeared to Thomas on a Monday or Tuesday or Wednesday, but instead, he chose to do it on the following first day of the week, on the eighth day. By doing so, our Lord gave his disciples a pattern they would follow in meeting with the risen Christ on the first day of the week in gathered worship. Just as God came and communed with Adam and Eve in the garden sanctuary of Eden on the seventh day, so too, the disciples would commune with their God on the eighth day.

RUTH AS THE NEW CREATION

This eighth-day pattern gives us insight into what's happening in the book of Ruth. The book of Ruth comes eighth in the canon. It signals a new beginning. Yes, the nation of Israel has collapsed under the judges and has sunk into the deepest pit of idolatry. Even the priests are lost. But God is going to bring about a new Israel, a new creation. And he's going to accomplish this new work through Ruth, Naomi, and especially Boaz. When you compare the ending of Judges to the ending of the book of Ruth, you can see the contrast. Judges ends with the declaration that there was no king in Israel, whereas the last word in the book of Ruth is simply a name, *David*. All the hopes of all Israel are summed up in that one name. That one name calls to mind Israel's ideal king. It answers the problem presented by the book of Judges' conclusion. Here is the gospel in the face of Judges' bad news. God has met the problem described in the book of Judges in this man, David, a name synonymous with kingship. The people had no king; now they do. They had forgotten Yahweh was their king; now they have a continual reminder, a human representative of Yahweh's divine Lordship. Ruth, then, shows us how God will go about solving Israel's idolatry problem. He gives them a ruler after his own heart.

The beginning of the monarchy points to an important transition in Israel's history. Rule by judge was fine for a period, but then the world of the judges collapsed on itself. The people needed something new – or more specifically, they needed *someone* new. They needed a king. They needed a king after God's own heart, so God gave them David.

Now, in its historical context, the book of Ruth also answers another set of problems related to David's kingship. David's kingship did not go unchallenged in Israel. It's not as though David became king and everyone fell in line under his regime. After all, many people were invested in Saul's kingship prior to David coming to the throne, and they certainly raised objections to David wearing the crown. In particular, there were questions about David's family background, as we will see. Ruth answers those challenges. In that sense, the book of Ruth is not just a work of history or even theology; it is a work of apologetics, designed to defend God's chosen king. Sometimes the best way to defend the truth is with a story.

THE CHALLENGE TO DAVID'S KINGSHIP

What were some of the objections to Davidic rule in ancient Israel? First, David was the descendant of an illegitimate union. In Genesis 38, Judah's sons failed to keep the levirate law (cf. Deut. 25:5ff). Judah's oldest son, Er, had married Tamar, but he died before producing a male offspring. Under the levirate provision, his brother was to take Tamar to himself and raise up a male offspring through her to replace the deceased. But Onan refused to fulfill his duty and was struck dead (Gen. 38:3-10). Judah told Tamar to wait on another son, Shelah, to grow up but had no intention of giving Shelah as a levir. When Tamar realized Judah's family had abandoned her, she used deception.[3] Tamar tricked Judah into fulfilling the levirate duty with her on his own. When it is revealed that Tamar was now pregnant through Judah, Judah realized how wicked he had been by failing to provide for Tamar. Judah both admits that God was indeed righteous in striking his sons dead, and also that Tamar was more righteous than he. Nothing in the story condemns Tamar for her actions; she wanted

---

3   This is fitting with the frequent pattern in the Old Testament of righteous women fighting tyrannical men by using deception, such as Rebekah, the Egyptian midwives, Jael, and Rahab.

to preserve the seed line and her place in the covenant people. We have to read this story in terms of redemptive history and the promised messianic line, rather than making decontextualized moral judgments. But that does not negate the fact that, because of Judah's sin, the son who is born to Tamar is illegitimate. Insofar as Tamar intended to gain a rightful heir to take Er's place, she was in the right; but insofar as Judah was doing nothing more than satisfying his lusts, he brought shame to his family. Thus, the son born of the Tamar/Judah union, Perez, is a bastard and is regarded as such in terms of the law.

Note a couple of things here. First, it is the failure of the family of Judah to perform the levirate duty that causes the tribe of Judah to fall into shame. We will find in the book of Ruth that the tribe of Judah is redeemed, exalted, and preserved because of a fulfillment of the levirate duty. Boaz plays the role of a levir husband to Ruth (and by extension to Naomi). He is the true Judah.

But, second, consider Deut. 23:2 in this connection: "No one born of a forbidden union may enter the assembly of the Lord. Even to the tenth generation, none of his descendants may enter the assembly of the Lord." The "assembly of the LORD" in this context refers to political rule. When the law says, he shall not "enter the assembly of the Lord," it does not mean that they could not participate in synagogue life, but they did not have full citizenship and certainly could not hold any kind of office in the commonwealth of Israel to the tenth generation. For Judah's family, this period of exclusion begins with Perez. But look at the genealogy at the end of the book. What a curious way to end such a sweet, romantic tale. How odd. Some have even wondered if the genealogy serves any real purpose at all in the story; it seems to be inexplicably tacked on at the end of the book. But keep in mind Genesis 38 and Deuteronomy 23, and count the generations beginning in Ruth 4:18:

1. Perez
2. Hezron
3. Ram
4. Amminadab

5. Nahshon
6. Salmon
7. Boaz
8. Obed
9. Jesse
10. David

There are ten generations from Perez to David. Do you want to see how the law of God and the promise of God come together? God had promised to the tribe of Judah that the scepter would not depart from his household (Gen. 49:10). That is to say, the tribe of Judah would produce the king over Israel. Judah was the royal tribe. And yet, because of Judah's sin, and the law of Deut. 23:2, no son of the tribe of Judah could be king until the tenth generation. How will this conflict be resolved? The end of Ruth shows us. In the first eligible Judahite generation, David's generation, a son of Judah is made king. The blessing in Gen. 49:10 is fulfilled without violating Deut. 23:2.

This also sheds light on Israel's demand for a king in 1 Samuel 8. What's so bad about Israel wanting a king in 1 Samuel 8? There's nothing wrong with having a king. It was promised already that the tribe of Judah would produce a king to reign over Israel. In Deuteronomy 17, Moses looked ahead and gave laws pertaining to kingship. It is obvious God wanted his people to have a king *when the time was right.* But Israel's request for a king came at a time where there weren't any eligible sons who could fulfill that office. The sons of Judah were excluded to the tenth generation. Thus, Israel is asking for a king prematurely – and they should have known that. When they ask for a king in 1 Samuel 8, the problem is not that they want a king; it's that they want a king before it's time. They want a king who will be given to them in violation of God's promise and God's law. They should have known there was simply no way things could have worked out with Saul, the Benjaminite. The nation of Israel seized kingly glory prematurely the same way Adam and Eve did.

But there was a second objection to David's kingship over Israel. He had foreign blood in his veins. Now, this objection can't be answered quite so neatly as the one we just dealt with, but there is an answer. According to Deut. 17:15, no foreigner was to be enthroned as king over Israel. Further, in Deut. 23:3f (right next to the verse prohibiting illegitimate sons from full citizenship rights), Moabites are forbidden citizenship in Israel to the tenth generation because they refused to provide bread and water for the Israelites in the wilderness. The Moabites cursed rather than blessed. David was clearly the tenth generation descendant from Ruth, who was a Moabitess. So what gives? How can David be king? The book of Ruth shows us a way around Deut. 23:3f. Ruth was a convert. Ruth was brought into the covenant line by God's grace and by her faithfulness to her mother-in-law. Ruth is grafted into the covenant people through a legal levirate marriage and is given God's blessing to prove it. Her marriage and her grafting into Israel are in line with Old Testament law. And so the book of Ruth shows that Ruth wasn't a Moabitess anymore. She traded in her identity as a Moabitess in order to become a member of Israel. She said to Naomi, "Your God will be my God and your people will be my people." She leaves behind the old Moabite family to enter into the new family of Israel. This transformation is later sealed in her marriage to an Israelite man named Boaz; by marriage she is incorporated in the family and line of Boaz. She becomes a member of Israel; indeed, she becomes a member of the royal seed line. Instead of being an obstacle to David's kingship, we can actually say she paved the way for it. In fact, perhaps more than anyone else in the Old Testament, she shows us what it means to have the faith of Abraham, to be a true Jew as Paul identifies in Romans 2: she does not possess the law by nature but does the things of the law by faith.

The book of Ruth, then, defends David and his lineage as God's choice to rule Israel, which, of course, leads ultimately to Jesus. In Matthew's genealogy, Ruth is one of a select few women who are included in that genealogy leading to the birth of Christ.[4] Not only does David come from her, but the Greater David, the Greater Boaz, Jesus, comes from her.

⸺◈⸺

THE MESSIANIC KINGDOM

We can already begin to see some of the ways in which Ruth applies to our lives today. It doesn't do us a lot of good to talk about the purpose of the book unless we translate it into practice. Just as there were challenges to David's rightful rule, so there are challenges to the rightful reign of King Jesus. And so we have to defend his kingship, even as the book of Ruth defended the kingship of David. The book of Ruth is a lesson in apologetics. One of the best ways to defend the gospel is through storytelling. Through the art of a captivating narrative, we can show the beauty and the glory of how God brought everything together in Christ. All God's purposes for creation are brought to a climax and to culmination in Jesus. Ruth gives us a glimpse of that.

Defending faith in Christ is not just a matter of arguments and syllogisms. Many times, it's a matter of telling stories. We need to learn to tell the story of the gospel to our culture in such a way that the gospel story exposes what is wrong with our culture and sets things right. The Apostle Peter says that we are to give an answer for the hope that we have. We are to live our lives in such a way that we provoke questions on the part of non-Christian onlookers. Our lives are to demonstrate hope. When they ask about the hope that we have, we are to be ready to give an answer. We are to have a ready-made defense for why we have the hope that we do. Ruth is a helpful model: it showed why the Israelites were right to hope in David and submit to his reign. While the challenges we face in defending Jesus' reign are not identical to those brought against David's reign, Ruth shows us an effective apologetic strategy.

---

4   Interestingly, Tamar is another woman named in Matthew's genealogy. Both women were Gentile outsiders, grafted into Judah, and both women needed levirate husbands.

Whoever wrote the book of Ruth was answering on behalf of the Davidic hope. If the question of the day was, "What right do you have to hope in King David?" the book of Ruth gives an answer. And if the question today is, "What right do we have to hope in King Jesus?" we must give an answer that declares Jesus is the fulfillment of all God's purposes, and he has brought in a new world.

THE SOLUTION: THE GOSPEL ACCORDING TO RUTH

What exactly is the gospel according to Ruth? Ruth shows the world just what she needs. In this book, the situation of Naomi and Ruth is emblematic of Israel's situation. Where are Naomi and Ruth at the beginning of the book? They are without a king; they are without a husband; they are left desolate, destitute, and desperate. Where are they at the end of the book? Fulfilled, cared for, protected. The story of Ruth is proof that God will not abandon his covenant bride but will provide for her, ultimately by giving her a greater Boaz and a greater David, a greater Kinsman-Redeemer, and a greater King. What does Israel need? She needs a king, but not one like Elimelech and Saul; she needs a king like Boaz and David. Of course, our situation is like that of Israel/Naomi/Ruth as well. The world is lost, without a king and without hope. What does the world need? The Greater Boaz, the Greater David. The world needs King Jesus. The world needs a kinsman-redeemer, one who can do for us what we cannot do for ourselves, who will provide for us, protect us, and care for us. Ruth is a blueprint of the gospel; the gospel fulfills the types and shadows found in the book of Ruth.

It's very interesting to see how enthralled Americans are with royalty. Sure, our nation was premised on the rejection of monarchy. We fought a war to free ourselves from the tyranny of King George. But we cannot escape the appeal of royalty. It resonates with something deep inside us. One of the most popular movies of all time is *The Return of the King*, the third in the *Lord of the Rings* trilogy. Why is that? Why are we so fascinated with kingship? God has made us in such a way that we crave kingship. Sin distorts our desire for the right kind of king, but the desire persists. The reason so many fairy tales revolve around good kings defeating bad kings, or the good king rescuing and taking the bride to himself, or the "Return of the King" motif, is that we were made for precisely this kind of story. We never get tired of this kind of story. God designed the human soul and human history to match one another. The human soul longs for the kind of king God has sent into the world. His name is Jesus. He is our king.

1

THE EXILE OF ELIMELECH

Ruth 1:1-5

In the days when the judges ruled there was a famine in the land, and a man of Bethlehem in Judah went to sojourn in the country of Moab, he and his wife and his two sons. ² The name of the man was Elimelech and the name of his wife Naomi, and the names of his two sons were Mahlon and Chilion. They were Ephrathites from Bethlehem in Judah. They went into the country of Moab and remained there. ³ But Elimelech, the husband of Naomi, died, and she was left with her two sons. ⁴ These took Moabite wives; the name of the one was Orpah and the name of the other Ruth. They lived there about ten years, ⁵ and both Mahlon and Chilion died, so that the woman was left without her two sons and her husband.

Viewing the structure of the book, we find that Ruth is divided into four sections, which correspond nicely. This is one of those rare biblical books where the chapter divisions actually fit very well with the flow of the story. Ruth 1 shows *the need* for a kinsman-redeemer. Ruth 2 reveals *the search* and longing for a kinsman-redeemer. Ruth 3 delivers *the promise* of a kinsman-redeemer. And then in Ruth 4, finally, we find *the accomplishment* of the kinsman-redeemer. Everything hinges on this kinsman-redeemer. And, of course, everything in this story is symbolic and typological. What Boaz does for Ruth and Naomi is emblematic of what God does for Israel and the church through Jesus Christ. We are dead and need the one who can make us alive. We are lost and need the one who can find us. We are impoverished and need the one who can enrich us. We are homeless and need the one who can make us a dwelling place. We are hungry and need the one who can feed us.

The opening scene in Ruth 1:1-5 is critical because it sets up the whole narrative. Everything flows out of what happens in these information-packed verses. If you think of Ruth as a kind of drama, verses 1-5 put the actors in their places.

The Importance of Names

The names of people and places reveal a great deal. Names are highly significant throughout the book of Ruth.[5] Etymology is often overused, and sometimes the meaning of names is not as certain as we might like. We should not make etymology decisive in the interpretation of a passage, but etymology can enrich our reading of a text.

We are told that this family is from Bethlehem. *Bethlehem* means "house of bread," which points us back to the original place of free and abundant food, the Garden of Eden. In Genesis 2, emphasis is placed on the availability of food. The garden is replete with trees. It is a house of food. Bethlehem is a new house of food in Israel. It's intended to be a new Eden. This is not much of a stretch because we know this was, in some sense, true of the promised land as a whole. When God tells Israel that he will give them a land flowing with milk and honey, he is indicating that

---

5   Namelessness also is important in the book of Ruth.

the land itself is a new Edenic environment. But the situation in the book of Ruth presents a problem: a famine has hit Israel, even Bethlehem. The house of bread is empty. The land flowing with milk and honey now faces shortages.

The dissonance between Bethlehem's name and its situation can only mean one thing: the land is under a curse. More specifically, the people of the land are under a curse. The land is dead, meaning the people are dead, too. The land's famine correlates to the people's famine. They have forsaken Yahweh and thus are hungry for true food. We need to understand that famines don't just happen. They are not random, "chance" events. Whether this famine was due to drought or warfare (the latter is more likely, given the Midianite invasion), it was a chastisement from God.

God had promised to make Bethlehem a house full of bread, overflowing with food. If that isn't happening, if the promises aren't coming to fulfillment, then there is a problem. The problem cannot be that God is unfaithful; the problem must be that Israel has sinned. And that is exactly what we find.

We are told the story takes place during the time when the judges reigned in Israel. The book of Judges explains why God is bringing famine against the land. Elimelech should have reasoned something like this: "If there's a famine here in the bread basket, this must mean God is angry with us, and God must have good reason for his anger, and so the solution to the famine is for us to repent." Throughout Scripture, whenever disasters hit, these tragic events are occasions for repentance. Indeed, even when disasters are not directly linked to some particular sin, they are reminders that we must continually turn from sin to serve the living God. There is not always a one-to-one correspondence between disasters that strike our lives and some particular act of sin, but any event that reveals the fallenness of the world must be viewed as an occasion for repentance. Elimelech does not reason in this way. Instead of repenting, he runs. Instead of turning to God, he turns to Moab.

The little town of Bethlehem usually prompts positive associations for the biblical reader. When we hear of Bethlehem, we automatically think of Christmas and everything associated with that joyous event. But Bethlehem did not have such pleasant associations at the time of Ruth. The town was the death place of Rachel, the bride of the covenant, in Gen. 35:19. In Judges 17 and 19, Bethlehem is associated with the grossest forms of idolatry and immorality. Bethlehem, at least at this time in history, is a place marked by unfaithfulness, idolatry, and immorality. Elimelech does nothing to change that. In fact, he seems to be a part of Bethlehem's problem.

Attention to the names of the people in the book of Ruth sheds further light on the situation. In the Bible, names were not chosen simply for aesthetic reasons; rather, they revealed that person's character and purpose. The closest analogy we may be familiar with are Indian names, which usually served as nicknames to reveal something about the person. Or, if you've read any of Flannery O'Connor's stories, you've no doubt noticed that she uses names in a highly symbolic way to reveal the inner character of a person. While there are some questions about the precise etymology of some of the names in Ruth 1, understanding their meanings contributes to our overall understanding of the story.

The name Elimelech means "God is King," which is highly ironic given the situation. Remember, Elimelech lives in the time of the judges, a time when "there was no king in Israel, and everyone did what was right in his own eyes." Elimelech's name should have reminded him that Yahweh (or El) was his king, but he failed to submit to Yahweh. Instead, he did what was right in his own eyes. So Elimelech failed to live up to his name. In other words, he was a hypocrite. When Elimelech led his family out of the land of promise, away from the place where God dwelt among his people, he was sinning against the true King of heaven and earth. He failed to repent of his sin and trust in the Lord as his King.

Elimelech's wife is Naomi. Her name means "pleasant." Her name also takes on an ironic and contradictory twist because, for Naomi, life is anything but pleasant. She is driven away from her homeland by famine and loses all three men in her life. She is surrounded by death on every side. Thus, toward the end of Ruth 1, she changes her name to match her situation. She renames herself "Mara," which means "bitter," because life has become bitter for her. She is no longer living a "pleasant" life, but a "bitter" life. Dealing with her sorrow and tragedy is what drives the book's narrative.

Of course, by the end of the story, Naomi's bitterness has returned to pleasantness. Her name changes but ultimately changes back again. Tracing her name is a way of tracing the plot of the whole book. And of course, there are deeper dimensions to her changing situation. God's dealings with Naomi are emblematic of God's dealings with Israel (and the church, as the new Israel). In other words, what God does through Naomi and for her and around her is symbolic and typological of God's treatment of Israel. In many ways, Naomi is more central to the story than Ruth is (made more obvious in the Hebrew than in English translations). This book could have been named after Naomi just as fittingly as it was named after Ruth. Naomi is the focal point of both loss and gain, of death and new life. Naomi is the bride of the covenant. She is the one left stranded as a childless widow because of the apostasy of her husband. She's left empty, helpless, and hopeless. Ruth 1:3 actually suggests her central, pivotal position in the narrative: "But Elimelech, the husband of Naomi, died, and she was left with her two sons." The focus of this text is on her — her husband, her sons, her triple loss. We get the sense from these opening verses that this story is going to be told from her perspective. Indeed, when we look at this story through her eyes, we truly see the saving grace of God as Naomi is saved from death and brought into new life. God is not going to leave Naomi stranded in exile in Moab, helpless and husbandless. He is going to redeem and restore her — and in doing so, he shows he is determined to rescue Israel.

Throughout the story, Ruth becomes more and more closely linked with Naomi so that by the end of the story whatever happens to one of them happens to the other. As the story progresses, Ruth takes more and more opportunities to act in Naomi's place. Their roles in the story ultimately merge into one. When Ruth gets remarried, it's functionally Naomi's remarriage, and the son of Ruth and Boaz takes the place of Naomi's deceased husband.

The names of Elimelech's sons are not exactly flattering. Chilion means something like "ailing" or "pining." His name could carry the sense of pining for the land while he's away from it, or it could mean that he's wasting away because of some kind of illness that leads to his death. Mahlon means "perishing." It's a fitting name for him not only because he perishes but because his family's name is in danger of perishing. It's unlikely that the parents actually gave these names to their sons. These could be nicknames given to them later, perhaps even by the inspired author.[6]

The names of these sons also are fitting since they both die almost immediately in the story. Their names suggest not only Israel's vulnerable position but the threat of the curse hanging over the nation. These two young men are taken away from the land of promise; cut off from God's presence and God's people, they are doomed to waste away and perish.

But there's more. The Hebrew word used to describe the sons is a very specific term. It could probably best be translated as "lads." The word shows up again at the end of the story to describe Ruth's baby, Obed. Clearly then, Obed is going to take the place of the deceased sons; he is raised up as their substitute to claim their inheritance and carry on the family name.

Some scholars think Ruth's name means "friendship," which is fitting given the role she plays in this story. Her sister-in-law's name, Orpah, is related to the word for "back of the neck." Her

---

6   Alternative names are given to Saul's sons, as becomes evident if we compare 1-2 Kings to 1-2 Chronicles.

name may mean she is "stiff-necked," because she refuses to bow to Israel's God the way that Ruth does. Or it could mean that she turns her back on Naomi. Either way, the names of the two women form a sharp contrast. Whereas Ruth has befriended Naomi, Orpah turns her back on Naomi and leaves her.

Elimelech's family members are identified as Ephrathites, which is probably a clan name (cf. 1 Sam. 17:12). It likely means they are descendants of Caleb and indicates they were an aristocratic family. This was a prominent family in the region, so to be driven out by famine would have been a big deal. One commentator says this would have been like saying the Vanderbilts have suddenly become poor sharecroppers.

From Israel to Moab

Due to the famine, this family leaves the land of promise and heads to Moab. This is a surprising destination, to say the least. The Moabites had a very poor reputation in redemptive history, having been no friend of the Israelite nation. In fact, they had been some of the Israelites' staunchest enemies.

Where did Moab come from? How did these people trace their roots? Questions like these are not just Bible trivia; they actually shed a lot of light on what's going on in the story. Descendants of Lot, Moab was related to Israel by blood. But Moab was born out of an incestuous relationship between Lot and one of his daughters.

Given their origins, it is not surprising that the people of Moab were given over to sexual sin. The Moabites were known for their shameless immorality in the service of their god Chemosh. In Numbers 25, Moabite women led the Israelites into harlotry and apostasy. And when Israel was on her way to the promised land, Moab refused to give Israel bread and water but instead hired Balaam to pronounce a curse on Israel.

So picture the situation. When Israel was in a famine-like situation, trekking through the wilderness, and needed bread and water, they looked to Moab to help, but Moab cursed rather than blessed. On top of that, Moabite women were already known to lead Israelite men astray. Given that background, think about the decision facing Elimelech. His family is hungry. His sons are growing up and need wives. Why does Elimelech choose to take his family into a region known for refusing to give Israelites bread? Why does he go into a region where the women are known to entice the Israelite men into sin? This is a treacherous act on Elimelech's part — and he will pay for his folly.

⚜

LACK, LACK LIQUIDATED

Ruth is a masterful story with an exquisite literary structure. Known for his classic study of folk tales, Vladimir Propp observed that folk stories often have the same basic structure: lack, lack liquidated, or need, need-met. Think about Cinderella. Early in the story, Cinderella finds herself under the thumb of her wicked stepmother. What she lacks is a good home. She needs to be rescued from her step-mother's cruelty. By the end of the story, her lack is liquidated and her need met. Ruth is going to work in a similar way. The opening verses show us what's lacking. The needs of the main feminine characters are going to be met, one by one, until we come to the end of the story and the reversal of fortune is complete.

What are the needs identified in these opening lines of the story? First, there is famine in the bread basket; there is hunger. By the end of Ruth 1, the famine is over, and in Ruth 2, we find God making abundant provision for Ruth and Naomi through Boaz. The lack of bread will be liquidated.

Secondly, there's the lack of a home. Elimelech's family leaves the promised land and goes into a self-imposed exile. Later, Naomi and Ruth return to the land and find a home there. Ultimately, they will find rest in Boaz, who brings them into his own family.

Finally, there is the lack of an heir. The two sons died childless, leaving behind two widows. Again, by the end of the story, everything needed will be provided. Ruth will find a husband better than the one who died. Through him, she will have a son to take the place of the deceased. Boaz and Obed liquidate the lack of men earlier in the story.

The book of Ruth moves from emptiness to fullness, from death to resurrection life, from bitterness to joy, and from exile to restoration. We could even say it is a story from "Mara" to "Naomi," from bitterness to pleasantness.

A FAMINE OF RIGHTEOUSNESS

The famine happens because of sin. Death comes to Elimelech and his sons because of sin. Famine is specifically singled out as a form of judgment on Israel in Leviticus 26 and Deuteronomy 28: it is a sign of God's anger against the covenant people. God reveals to the Israelites how his special relationship with them will work. When they start to see the curses of the covenant come upon them — such as diseases or famine — they should get busy repenting. If they do not repent, they will be removed from the land altogether.

By taking his family into exile, Elimelech, in a sense, imposes upon himself the ultimate curse of the covenant. He is driven out of the land where God had put his name and his presence. It is very hard to avoid the conclusion that when Elimelech left the land, at least under these circumstances, he was sinning. True, Abraham also left the land because of famine, but that happened before the land was given to Abraham's family as a settled possession. When Elimelech leaves the land, his departure is a sign that something has gone wrong. You could say he followed his stomach rather than his faith. Instead of restoring food to the bread basket through repentance, he takes what looks like an easy way out by going to Moab. Who knows what compromises were entailed in his decision? Where would they worship the true God? What kind of community could they hope to find? Elimelech seems to be doing as he pleases rather than what is right. And that may be why all the men in the family die in Moab, a punishment for Elimelech's sin. They chose exile from the land and ended up being exiled from the face of the earth.

Elimelech did not wait for God to drive him from the land; he chose to leave on his own. Rather than begging the Lord for mercy, he turned to the Moabites for mercy. We cannot say with certainty that by crossing the boundaries of the promised land Elimelech became a full blown apostate, but it certainly looks that way. If this is not covenant breaking, it's very close. If we were to translate Elimelech's action into a New Covenant scenario, it's as though Elimelech left the church. He left the fellowship of God's people and the place where God had put his name. It's a self-excommunication.

THE CHURCH AS THE SPHERE OF LIFE

The lesson for us is clear: Do not be an Elimelech. Do not forsake the place and people of God. We live in a time when many people look at the church and do not see much value there. The church does not impress them. But think about it: if you looked at the land of promise in the days of Elimelech, it didn't look like much either. What's so great about this land? There's a famine here. What's so great about the church? It seems like there's very little fruit being borne. God often works in hidden and surprising ways. We must learn to submit to God's plan and pattern for us. We must learn to submit to God's judgments and not run to the Moabs of the world for help. We need to trust God, repent, pray for our daily bread, and keep walking with the Lord and his people. We must seek God where he has promised to be found. For Elimelech that meant in the local assemblies, the synagogues, scattered throughout the land of Israel and meeting each Sabbath (Lev. 23:3). For us, it means not forsaking the assembling of the saints (Heb. 10:25). As soon as something bad happened, Elimelech jumped ship and headed for Moab. When bad things happen to us, we are tempted to run from God and run from the church. But this is precisely what we must not do. Instead, we should run to the church. We should run into God's presence by claiming the blessings that he has promised to make available to us in the midst of his people. We must plead with him to grant us repentance and to bless us instead of curse us.

Elimelech is, in a sense, already under the curse of famine in the land, but by leaving the land he intensifies the curse, and the famine escalates into death. Outside of the church, outside of the place where God has promised to make himself present through the means of grace (Word and sacrament), there is nothing but death. If you leave the sphere of life, you enter the sphere of death.

LEAVING THE LAND

Some people might defend Elimelech and object to such a negative interpretation, saying, "A man must do what is necessary to feed his family. Leaving the land was perfectly understandable." The counterpoint to that line of reasoning is simple. Obviously, not everybody in Bethlehem left the land, yet they still managed to survive. Boaz certainly did not see the need to take his family out of the land, and yet his family did not starve to death.

A more potent objection is: "Abraham left the land of promise during the time of famine and Jacob did so as well. Why can't we say Elimelech is just imitating the actions of the patriarchs? Isn't Elimelech just repeating the actions of Abraham and Jacob? There seems to be no divine disapproval of the actions of Abraham and Jacob." But this argument fails to deal with key differences between the situation of the patriarchs and the situation of Elimelech. Abraham and Jacob may have left the land promised to them because of famine, but the land of promise remained unconquered. Abraham did not dwell in the land as a permanent resident. He knew he was just a sojourner. And it is the same with Jacob. Both men knew it would be centuries and generations before their descendants came into full possession of the land. The sins of the Canaanites had to rise to the full measure before they would be driven out of the land. Their land would belong to Israel as long as she was faithful. But the full inheritance of the land had not yet happened in the time of Abraham and Jacob.

They left before the conquest of the land and before God set his name there. So for the patriarchs to leave the land does not carry the same significance as when Elimelech leaves the land.

Abraham's return to the land is also worth noting. In Genesis 12-13, it is true that Abraham leaves the land because of famine, but he is not blessed until he turns back to the land. *Then* he leaves Egypt with spoil. It is as if Abraham's departure from the land was a kind of exile. But when he turns back toward the land, it is an exodus complete with plunder from the Egyptians.

THE LAND THEME

To fully understand the dynamic of Ruth 1, it is important for us to trace the theme of the land. From the very first promise of land in Scripture, all the way through the glorified new creation, God's covenant is tied to the earth (*Appendix A* has an extensive treatment of the Theology of the Land). The creation is the arena in which redemption takes place; the creation is the stuff God uses to bring about redemption, and the stuff of creation is redeemed.

We have a tendency to think of the Christian hope as something that takes us out of the creation as if redemption means escaping this world. But that is actually far more Platonic (or even Gnostic) than it is Christian. The biblical hope is anchored to the earth and creation. It is *this* world that is fallen; it is *this* world that suffers sin's curse; it is *this* earth that must be redeemed. Otherwise, Satan has won the victory. If creation is not redeemed, Satan has claimed creation for himself and God let him have it.

But the biblical narrative gives redemption a *this-worldly* focus. In the biblical narrative, redemption means God is counterclaiming what Satan has claimed for himself. God placed the curse on the world and God can lift the curse on the world. God can repeal the curse and replace it with blessing.

This truth has huge implications for how we live our lives and how we think about the future. All too often, we think of the future Christian hope as heaven. But what we usually think of as heaven is not our final destination. Rather, it is what theologians call "the intermediate state." It is true that the soul of the believer goes to be with the Lord in heaven at death and that is a glorious thing (Phil. 1:23), but it is not the end of the story. The soul awaits its final redemption and the resurrection of the body at the last day. When our bodies are raised, the creation itself will be glorified. If our future hope terminates in heaven, then we are Platonic rather than Pauline. Plato said the body is a prison house for the soul, and at death, the soul is released so it can float upward into an ethereal realm.

This Platonic vision of salvation has had far too much influence on Christian thought, practice, and piety. The Christian hope is certainly heavenly, but it is also *this-worldly*. It's about the resurrected body dwelling in a new heaven and earth for all eternity. Our hope is *future*-worldly, but it is not other-worldly. It is this world that is going to be redeemed. The body you now have will be the body you inhabit for all eternity (albeit, in glorified form). This is the Christian hope: the very body that has borne the curse of sin and suffered for the sake of the Savior will now bear the full weight of blessing and glory and splendor and majesty. It may not seem like this has much to do with the book of Ruth, but it does. The book of Ruth not only teaches salvation by grace, it teaches a comprehensive salvation.

2

MAKING COVENANT WITH FOREIGNERS

Ruth 1:1-5

In the days when the judges ruled there was a famine in the land, and a man of Bethlehem in Judah went to sojourn in the country of Moab, he and his wife and his two sons. ² The name of the man was Elimelech and the name of his wife Naomi, and the names of his two sons were Mahlon and Chilion. They were Ephrathites from Bethlehem in Judah. They went into the country of Moab and remained there. ³ But Elimelech, the husband of Naomi, died, and she was left with her two sons. ⁴ These took Moabite wives; the name of the one was Orpah and the name of the other Ruth. They lived there about ten years, ⁵ and both Mahlon and Chilion died, so that the woman was left without her two sons and her husband.

In Moab, Elimelech's sons came of age and took Moabite wives to themselves. Was this a sin? The Bible does not forbid interracial or interethnic marriage, but it does forbid interreligious or intercovenantal marriage (2 Cor. 6:14). There is a reason to think, given prior history, that just as Elimelech made a mistake in seeking bread in Moab (cf. Deut. 23:3-6), his sons also should not have sought wives from Moab. Is this a case of history repeating itself? Numbers 25 records a great fiasco in Israel's history, when Israelite men committed fornication with Moabite women. As a result, God struck dead 24,000 Israelite men. The same kind of thing happens here, albeit on a smaller scale. There is no hint of fornication in Ruth 1, but there is also no reason to think the Moabite women converted to faith in the Lord when they entered into marriage with Mahlon and Chilion. The result? The two Israelite men are struck dead in judgment. They are executed for marrying outside the covenant. Though there is no indication of fornication, it seems there is a violation of the sanctity of the covenant.

God told his people in the book of Deuteronomy that, "when the Lord your God delivers them [that is, the Canaanites] over to you, and you defeat them, then you must devote them to complete destruction" (Deut. 7:2). God specifically forbade his people from entering into a covenant with the Canaanites. Obviously, this would apply to pagans living outside the land of promise as well. God says his people are not to enter into deep covenant relationships with unbelievers. Deut. 22:10 teaches the same principle in a symbolic law: "You shall not plow with an ox and a donkey together." Why does God give his people this law? It is not that farmers were tempted to plow with an ox and a donkey yoked together. The animals would just end up going in circles because of their height and size differences. Rather, the point of the law is to show Israel how incongruent and fruitless it would be to yoke herself to unclean nations and people. The ox is a sacrificial animal and the donkey is not; they must not be yoked together. Israel must not enter into deep covenant fellowship with those who are outside the covenant.

These laws did not prohibit Israel from befriending foreigners or strangers who happened to be passing through the land. These laws did not prohibit hospitality, mercy ministry, or evangelism. The Israelites were not forbidden to eat with Gentiles, though the

Jews eventually set up further hedges between themselves and the Gentiles that made meal sharing impossible. But these laws did mean that the Israelites could not enter into deep covenant bonds with a pagan, such as marriage. If a pagan converts to faith in the Lord and is integrated into the covenant community, then marriage is lawful. Otherwise, it is not.

So, it is likely the sons of Elimelech have unequally yoked themselves to Moabite women. There is no indication they required Orpah and Ruth to convert before marriage. The sons' actions here differ from those of Moses, who took an Ethiopian bride, or Samson, who, under the leading of the Spirit, offered marriage to a Philistine woman while also calling on her to transfer loyalty to God's people.

Therefore, rather than converting Orpah and Ruth to faith in the Lord, Elimelech's family became syncretistic while in Moab.[7] They most likely retained many of their Israelite customs and practices while "doing as the Moabites do while in Moab." They likely incorporated worship of the Moab god Chemosh into their family piety. How else could they have gotten bread and land to farm from the Moabites? So, if anything, the transfer of loyalty is headed in the wrong direction. Instead of converting the Moabites to their faith, the true faith, they are being converted to a false faith.

At the end of the first section, the men are dead. Elimelech, Mahlon, and Chilion are judged. Naomi has been left stranded, an Israelite in a foreign land. Her husband led her into sin by leaving the land and, as a consequence, death has reigned and the family of Elimelech faces extinction. The family name is in danger of perishing.

---

7   Syncretism is the blending of two or more religions.

A RAY OF HOPE
Ruth 1:6-7

⁶ Then she arose with her daughters-in-law to return from the country of Moab, for she had heard in the fields of Moab that the Lord had visited his people and given them food. ⁷ So she set out from the place where she was with her two daughters-in-law, and they went on the way to return to the land of Judah.

What happens next? Verses six and seven offer a ray of hope. The situation in Bethlehem has apparently changed. Bethlehem is no longer under God's discipline; God has visited his people and restored bread to the house of bread. The good news reaches Naomi while she's still dwelling in the region of Moab, and she and her two daughters-in-law begin a return to the land of promise.

Verse seven mentions the land of Judah, reminding us that the focus in the story is not Israel as a whole, but specifically the tribe of Judah. Remember, Judah came under a curse because he failed to require his sons to perform their levirate duties, which ends up leading to the birth of an illegitimate son named Perez (Gen. 38:29). And remember also that we know from the book of Deuteronomy that for ten generations the line of Judah is disqualified from full citizenship in Israel because of this sin of illegitimacy. The whole book of Ruth is going to hinge on the redemption and restoration of the tribe of Judah.

THE EXODUS/EXILE PATTERN
There is another important biblical pattern to notice. In the Scriptures, to leave the land is to undergo exile. To return to the land is to suffer an exodus. Abraham undergoes an exile/exodus in Genesis 12. He leaves the land because of famine, goes to Egypt,

then returns with spoil. God protects Abraham while he is in exile, plaguing Pharaoh when he seeks to attack Abraham's bride, and when Abraham departs, he does so with great treasure. Of course, this is a preview of what is to come in the book of Exodus itself. Abraham's experience will be repeated on a national scale. In Egypt, the entire nation will be attacked and enslaved by Pharaoh. Instead of attacking the bride, the Pharaoh (a serpent figure) will attack the seed of the bride by seeking to kill the Jewish baby boys. God will plague Pharaoh and then lead his people out of Egypt with tremendous plunder. There are many exile/exodus cycles in the Bible.

Indeed, the whole Bible can be read as the story of exile and exodus. Adam and Eve start off in the garden of Eden with access to the Tree of Life, but because they refuse to exercise patient faith they jump the gun and seize kingly privileges instead of waiting for God to bestow them. As a consequence of their sin, they are exiled from the Garden of Eden. The entire rest of the Bible then can be thought of as the story of God accomplishing an exodus for his people, restoring them to the sanctuary. The ultimate exile/exodus cycle happens at the cross. In Luke 9, Jesus is transfigured on the mount and begins to discuss his coming "exodus" with Moses and Elijah. How will it happen? He will be exiled on the cross — exiled from the city of Jerusalem, exiled from the community of Israel, exiled even, from his Father's presence. But then he returns (exodus) to the land of the living in his resurrection, and brings with him the ultimate plunder, namely, all the saints redeemed by his blood.

With all that in mind, it should be evident that geographic movement in the book of Ruth is not arbitrary. It is integral to the story. Ruth describes another exile/exodus cycle. However, the exodus in Ruth seems different. In these other cases, the exodus means bringing back great plunder, which does not appear to happen when Naomi begins her return to Judah. Peter Leithart notes the irregularity in Ruth 1:

In chapter one clearly we have an exodus pattern. Elimelech and Naomi leave the land, and Naomi returns with Ruth. But in many ways it is an unusual exodus. Instead of multiplying in the land of sojourning as Jacob did in Haran and Israel did in Egypt, Elimelech and his sons die, leaving Naomi with no seed. Instead of becoming enriched as Abraham, Isaac, Jacob, and Israel did, Elimelech and Naomi are impoverished. Jacob flees from Esau with only a staff and comes back with two wealthy companies; he goes out empty and comes back full. Naomi goes out full and comes back empty. Though Naomi is back in the land there has been no exodus, no redemption. These contrast with the patriarchal exoduses, support the traditional rabbinic notion that Elimelech sinned in leaving the land.[8]

In Ruth 1, the exodus seems empty, that Naomi returns empty-handed. *Or does she?* She actually returns from Moab with at least one piece of plunder, namely, Ruth. Naomi says she's empty-handed at the end of Ruth 1, but we're going to find as this story unfolds that she's not empty-handed at all. Naomi went down to Moab with two sons. Toward the end of the book, she's going to say that Ruth has been more valuable to her than seven sons. At this stage, Naomi does not realize how God has blessed her. But she will.

Think how often we do the same thing as Naomi. We groan and complain, seeing only the dark underside of our situation. We fail to see the silver lining in the storm clouds that are gathered over us. This is Naomi's situation at this point in the story. She does not see what God has provided for her.

Although slightly different, this exodus event in Ruth 1 does fit with the biblical pattern after all. She comes back with the best plunder of all. She comes back with the very best that Moab has to offer, which is Ruth.

---

8   "No. 45: The Structures of Ruth," Biblical Horizons, accessed November 14, 2018, http://www.biblicalhorizons.com/biblical-horizons/no-45-the-structures-of-ruth/

Naomi as Anti-Evangelist
Ruth 1:8-13

But Naomi said to her two daughters-in-law, "Go, return each of you to her mother's house. May the LORD deal kindly with you, as you have dealt with the dead and with me. [9] The LORD grant that you may find rest, each of you in the house of her husband." Then she kissed them, and they lifted up their voices and wept. [10] And they said to her, "No, we will return with you to your people." [11] But Naomi said, "Turn back, my daughters; why will you go with me? Have I yet sons in my womb that they may become your husbands? [12] Turn back, my daughters; go your way, for I am too old to have a husband. If I should say I have hope, even if I should have a husband this night and should bear sons, [13] would you therefore wait till they were grown? Would you therefore refrain from marrying? No, my daughters, for it is exceedingly bitter to me for your sake that the hand of the LORD has gone out against me."

Why does Naomi try to discourage the two widows from going to Judah with her? She gives them two reasons. First, she says she cannot raise up sons for them to marry, because of her old age. Beyond that, she argues that even if she could miraculously give birth, even if she were like another Sarah and had her womb opened at a very old age, by the time the sons were grown up, Orpah and Ruth themselves would be too old for marriage. These seem like convincing arguments, especially in a culture in which a woman's welfare was tied to having a husband.

Naomi's apologetic is quite troubling, however, since she is sending these two women away from God and away from his people. She is turning them back to idolatry, back to the land of Moab, back to the worship of the false god Chemosh. Why is Naomi doing this? There is a long and venerable interpretation of this book that places all Naomi's actions in the best possible light. On that reading of the book, Naomi is testing the girls to see if

21

they are truly converted. She is calling on them to count the cost of discipleship, to see if they will forsake their old homeland and families.

But that does not seem to be the best interpretation. Rather, it appears Naomi is first and foremost freeing Ruth and Orpah from any obligations to her. If Ruth and Orpah do bind themselves to Naomi in some way, it will be entirely voluntary. More than that, what we see here is how faithless Naomi became in exile. She is hardened. Remember that when Elimelech went to Moab, he was taking his family away from the church and the presence of God. Naomi has been away from the people of God for quite some time now. As a result, it is not surprising that she has become an unfaithful representative of Yahweh. She has despaired, and in her despondency she drives away potential converts. She has given up hope. We see this at the end of the chapter where she changes her name from Naomi to Mara and says "Yahweh is against me." Naomi's attempts to send the widows away revealed her wish to give up on God. It is as if she says to them, "You might as well serve your god. Your god will probably treat you better than our God will treat you. Look at what our God did to my family and me."

Naomi may have also had pragmatic reasons for sending the women away, thinking perhaps it would be easier for one widow to find provisions than three. Once again, this would reveal a failure to trust God. Whatever the reasons, the bottom line is that she encourages them to return to a life of idolatry, rather than to venture into the land of promise.

Indeed, Naomi even contemplates the possibility that Ruth and Orpah could find rest in the land of Moab, but we know that the land of promise is the place of rest. It is as if she says to them, "Perhaps a Moabite man can give you the rest my sons could not. Perhaps Chemosh can grant you rest since the Lord has not."

————— ❦ —————

The Role of the Levirate Law in Ruth

In verse 11, we discover one of the major themes in the book of Ruth. When Naomi speaks of raising up sons for these two girls, she is pointing to the Old Testament levirate law, which we can find described in Genesis 38.Under levirate law, if a man died leaving a widow without children, his brother was obliged to marry the widow and to raise up a child for his deceased brother. The first child they had when they came together would take the place of the deceased brother. That child would take the deceased man's inheritance and carry on his family name. Naomi does not believe there is hope for a levirate marriage. It appears that Elimelech's house will, after all, come to an end. There were no sons raised up before Naomi's two sons, Mahlon and Chilion, died. Naomi is giving up hope that her husband's family will continue. There is no seed who can come and destroy the seed of the serpent for them, no one to reclaim them and redeem their lost estate. This is the bleakness of the situation.

Now Orpah comes to agree with Naomi that this is a hopeless situation. So Orpah leaves. The meaning of her name refers to the back of the neck, so it is no surprise when she turns her back on Naomi and goes back to Chemosh.

How can Orpah be blamed for doing this? After all, she has not received the best evangelical witness from the family of Elimelech. All this family has shown her is that they do not trust their God to take care of them. So why not go back with her? In fact, what Naomi has just told her is that she is just as likely to find rest in the home of a worshipper of Chemosh as she is in the land of promise. Nevertheless, we have to say Orpah is still responsible for turning away, and she does so to her eternal damnation. Whereas Ruth (whose name means "friend" or "companion") will go on with Naomi and find salvation, Orpah rejects that offer of salvation and turns back to the worship of an idol. She was close to salvation, but she let it slip away from her.

Some have wondered how Ruth could know to cling to Naomi and her people, and why she would be drawn in this direction if, after all, the witness from this family was not positive or clear. Ruth may have become part of an unfaithful family, but some remnants of true worship would still have lingered. Elimelech's family would have told the stories of Yahweh and the great exodus story and the conquest. She would have heard those stories. So when the Israelites came, she knew this was the true God they were serving, and she was ready to cast her lot with them, following this God and giving up the god of her people. She is living among the people who are unfaithful, yet she's picked up just enough true teaching to be converted and brought to faith.

NAOMI'S TRANSFORMATION

If we think of Naomi as a positive character all along, there's not much change that takes place in the story. Under such a reading, Naomi herself does not stand in need of redemption. However, the story makes more sense if there is a dynamic transformation that takes place.

Flannery O'Connor, in many ways the queen of storytellers, once said that all narratives are about conversion. In other words, stories worth telling are about redemption. If Naomi's not acting wicked at this point in the story, she does not need much redeeming. Those in the Calvinist tradition are prone to flatten out these Old Testament narratives, making them very static. For example, we'll say that Saul, in 1 Samuel 15, did not lose anything when the kingdom was taken from him because surely he was a wolf in sheep's clothing all along. The text says the Spirit was taken from him, but he must have never actually had the Spirit, so there wasn't any real big loss there. He disguised his unbelief and apostasy for a while, but it was no big fall from grace because he wasn't ever in grace to begin with. But the narrative itself reads very differently. It says Saul was a new man, given a new heart, had the Spirit and was adopted by God. But in I Samuel 15 he loses all that. This is the opposite story to the narrative type mentioned by Flannery O'Connor. It's a story about losing everything.

The story of Judas also could be understood in a similar, flattened way. We might say that Judas was a bad guy all along, so there wasn't any real apostasy. Judas was simply evil, but his true nature was not revealed until later. Now, to be sure, there were signs that suggest things were not quite right with Judas at times. But Judas was not some static figure. After all, none of the other disciples suspected him of betraying the master. He also was able to do everything the disciples could do, even perform miracles.

We might be tempted to read the book of Esther in a similar way. We think that Mordecai and Esther must have been righteous all along. But it seems clear that Mordecai and Esther were in very deep sin at the beginning of the book. They are compromised and unfaithful. They are refusing to bear witness to the true God and his covenant. Only when there's a great crisis in the middle of the story, when they are faced with death and extinction, do they repent and change their ways.

In this story, we are going to see the radical transformation of Naomi. We're going to see God work in her life in such a way that she is converted. Of course, it becomes all the more important when we see that Naomi herself is a type, symbol, or picture of the nation of Israel. It is the people of Israel who stand in need of conversion and redemption. If the book is about the redemption of Naomi, who represents the people of God, it is about our transformation and redemption as well.

We are inclined to assert that Naomi is in deep sin thoughYahweh will slowly draw her back to himself. He will transform her, just as he will with Israel.

Ruth 1:14-15

[14] Then they lifted up their voices and wept again. And Orpah kissed her mother-in-law, but Ruth clung to her. [15] And she said, "See, your sister-in-law has gone back to her people and to her gods; return after your sister-in-law."

Orpah has left; Ruth clings to Naomi. Orpah has chosen the false god and now Naomi says to Ruth, "Well, you go too." But Ruth refuses; she has faith. Nothing can stop her. She is determined to be a part of Israel and to be incorporated into the priestly people. She has picked up enough teaching along the way to know that Yahweh must be the true God and that his land is the place of blessing.

The word "cling" used to refer to Ruth's clinging to Naomi is the same term that is used in Gen. 2:24 for the marriage of Adam and Eve. A man and a woman are to leave their father and mother, and they are to cling to one another. Ruth is bonding herself by means of covenant to Naomi. Her choice is literally the exact opposite of Orpah's choice. Orpah returned to her people and to her gods, but Ruth turns to Naomi's God and to her people. She is leaving her homeland and her family behind to journey by faith to the land of promise.

INCORPORATION INTO A NEW COMMUNITY

Through Naomi, Ruth is joining herself to Israel. She is becoming an Israelite, so to speak. She's joining herself to the covenant people and the covenant God. At this point, we could say that Ruth knows better theology, even at this stage in her life than a lot of individualistic American Christians who think one can have a relationship with God apart from his people. Listen to Ruth's speech in verses 16-17:

Do not urge me to leave you or to return from following you. For where you go I will go, and where you lodge I will lodge. Your people shall be my people, and your God my God. [17] Where you die I will die, and there will I be buried. May the Lord do so to me and more also if anything but death parts me from you.

True conversion includes incorporation into the people of God. You cannot have one without the other. You cannot worship and serve this God without being joined to his people.

This pledge to Naomi forms a "till-death-do-us-part" bond. But actually, it is even stronger than that. She says not even death will separate them. "Even after you die, Naomi, I'm not going to leave your people or this land or stop serving this God." Not even death will put an end to this relationship. However strong the natural bonds of affection were between Ruth and mother-in-law, beneath that was her love for Israel's God.

The lone reference to burial is also important. In verse 17, she says, "Where you die, I will die, and there will I be buried." Even though Ruth is probably going to outlive Naomi by many years, she is not going to leave that place. She is openly rejecting Moab and Chemosh altogether. She is going to remain in Israel for the rest of her life. Ruth wants to be buried there, which, of course, points us back to other important burial events, like Genesis 23, where Abraham negotiates for some property within the confines of the land of promise to have a place to bury Sarah. Ruth wants to be buried in the promised land like Sarah and the other great patriarchs of Israel because she wants to rest in Christ.

Ruth also takes a self-maledictory oath. She asserts that nothing, not even death, will separate her from the church, God's people. If she breaks this promise, she will suffer the wrath of God. In other words, "May death happen to me and even more if I forsake this covenant."

There are other details in Ruth's speech, which need to be considered. She says to Naomi, "Wherever you lodge, there I will lodge." The irony here is that Naomi is homeless. Naomi doesn't have a place to lodge. So again you see her desire to be a part of the covenant people exceeds anything else. Ruth is going to follow Naomi no matter what. She is counting the cost. She'll even suffer to prove her faith and her love. She is confident — much more confident, in fact, than Naomi is at this point in the story — that God will provide for them. Naomi seems to have given up all hope, but Ruth can even speak of finding a place to lodge. She's looking ahead, and by faith she believes that God will provide for them one way or another. So in this way she is a model disciple.

For all she knows at this point, she is accepting widowhood and childlessness, which, again, was a remarkable tragedy for a woman in her day. She is still of marriageable age. She could have married and raised up children; she didn't have to do this. Naomi has already pointed out that there is no eligible *levir* — that she's aware of anyway — who can perform the levirate obligation. So it seems that Ruth is accepting widowhood and childlessness for the rest of her life.

OATHS AND SACRAMENTS IN THE NEW COMMUNITY

This speech is one that we would do well to translate into our situation, our relationship with God and with his people. In doing so, we have to acknowledge that this self-maledictory oath Ruth takes toward Naomi, her God, and her people is much like the oaths we are under as the people of God. We have all taken these similar self-maledictory oaths. Baptism is just such an oath. When we join the church through baptism, we pledge to be faithful to God. As the waters of baptism are poured over us, we are committing: "God, may you drown me in these same baptismal waters that have cleansed me if I'm not faithful to you." The Lord's Supper provides us with a similar example. At the Lord's table we commit ourselves to God and to his service. We commit ourselves to living in covenant fellowship with his people. But if we're unfaithful to that promise: "God, may my body and blood be torn apart, may I be ripped apart, in this same way if I'm not faithful to the obligations of this covenant." So, just like Ruth, we've made an irrevocable break with idolatry; there can be no turning back. We have to press on, willing to suffer as Ruth did.

Like Ruth, we may not be Jews after the flesh, but we have become true Jews because we have been grafted into the covenant line by grace through faith. Therefore, we must persevere in the covenant by grace through faith. <u>Ruth is a model disciple for us.</u> She would rather cling to Naomi, this homeless one, rather than return to idolatry and seek blessings there. She loves God more than anything else.

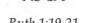

Ruth 1:19-21

So the two of them went on until they came to Bethlehem. And when they came to Bethlehem, the whole town was stirred because of them. And the women said, "Is this Naomi?" She said to them, "Do not call me Naomi; call me Mara, for the Almighty has dealt very bitterly with me. I went away full, and the LORD has brought me back empty. Why call me Naomi, when the LORD has testified against me and the Almighty has brought calamity upon me?"

THE RETURN OF NAOMI

There is quite a stir when Naomi finally makes it back to Bethlehem. She's been away about ten years, as we find back in Ruth 1:4. You can imagine what she would have looked like coming back, basically destitute, having lost a husband, two sons, and all means of support. The women ask, "Is this Naomi?" Rumors are floating through Bethlehem and there is no doubt that all that she has been through has taken a toll on her appearance. When they truly recognize her, she insists on a name change. She says, "Do not call me Naomi; call me Mara." That is, don't call me Mrs. Pleasant, call me Mrs. Bitter. In fact, we should think of these two names as antonyms. If you were to ask a Hebrew boy, "What is the opposite of Naomi?" he would have said, "Mara."

What should we make of her response in verses 20-21, where she describes the situation? What kind of speech is this? This speech is full of self-pity. It expresses a "woe is me" theology. Rather than confessing her sin, Naomi complains about how harsh and tyrannical God has been in dealing with her. She sees herself as a victim of God's severe providence. Unlike Ruth, Naomi uses the intimate covenant name for God, Yahweh, but it is clear she is thinking of God more as El Shaddai. She speaks of the Almighty a couple of times as though she wants to put this distance between her and God. By calling him El Shaddai, the Almighty One, she is saying God is this big, powerful bully and he is just pushing her around. Naomi does not seem to have any confidence in the goodness, graciousness, and kindness of God. Instead, it is as if she thinks that God is using all of his power against her. She portrays herself as a victim.

Some might say, "Isn't this kind of like Job?" Job complained against God and yet Job was vindicated. At the end of the book, Job makes speeches that make it sound like God has forsaken him, and he appears to be vindicated. Or you could look at the Psalter. There are plenty of places where the Psalmist cries out, "God, why have you forsaken me?" or "Why have I been cast down before you?" or "Why are you so distant from me?" Could we interpret Naomi's words in light of the book of Job or in light of the Psalter and perhaps reach a more positive reading? That's possible, and certainly believers do at times feel distant from God, and certainly sometimes feel as though God is against them. But Naomi's language goes beyond what we find in the book of Job or in the Psalter when we consider the broader contexts of those passages. Here Naomi is bitter and resentful. She appears to have lost all faith in God's goodness. We need to be sensitive to her plight, realizing what she has been through with the loss of the three men in her life. She at least recognizes that all this is God's doing. She understands that God is sovereign and that he is the one who has taken away her husband and her two sons. Nevertheless, she is hardly a model of faith. She refuses to realign herself with God's providence; she refuses to resign herself to God's will.

Two elements are missing at this stage in Naomi's life. The first is a confession of sin. She has been in sin, and she should have confessed it, and we do not see any indication of that at all. The other element is she seems totally oblivious to the great blessing that God has given to her in sending Ruth back with her. She thinks she has come back empty-handed. She suggests that she went out full and came back with absolutely nothing. When Ruth insisted on coming with Naomi, and when she saw that she was determined to go with her, she stopped speaking to Ruth. She ignored Ruth. Naomi wrote Ruth out of the story at this point and is paying no attention to God's provision of Ruth for her.

She fails to understand that she has had an exodus, that God has brought her out of Moab into the land with great plunder. In fact, she talks about losing her husband and her two sons, but we will find at the end of the book that she is going to say that having Ruth is better than having seven sons. If that is the case, of course, she is actually fuller now than when she left. She left with two sons and came back with one who's better than seven, which means she is plus five, in the ledger.

Ruth 1:22

> So Naomi returned, and Ruth the Moabite her daughter-in-law with her, who returned from the country of Moab. And they came to Bethlehem at the beginning of barley harvest.

Then finally, in verse 22, we read both a summary of all that has happened to this point and a preview of what's to come. First of all, it says "they" returned. Naomi may think of herself as having come back alone, but the narrator reminds us that she has Ruth with her. Naomi may think that she returned empty, but the narrator is not going to let us forget that she is not alone. In fact, there's a real grammatical oddity in the text. This comes through in most English translations.

In verse 22, Ruth is said to have *returned* to the land of promise. The same verb is used of Naomi, who once lived in the land of promise, left it, and then returns to it. How can Ruth return to the land of promise when she had never been there?

Why is it put this way? Ruth, even though she was not a Jew by nature, becomes a true Jew because of her faith. The text indicates that Ruth has finally found a place in which God can grant her rest. In verse 9, Naomi was sending Ruth back to Moab to find rest. But at the end of Chapter 1, we find that Ruth is now going to find rest in the land of promise. She's returning to it because spiritually speaking it is her true home. This is a homecoming for her because she belongs to Yahweh by faith. In a sense, we could say that Abraham's journey to the land of promise was a kind of homecoming even though he had never been there — it's where he belonged. The same can be said for Ruth.

Verse 22 also provides a preview of what is to come. At the very end of Chapter 1, the text says, "Now they came to Bethlehem at the beginning of the barley harvest." The chapter begins with a famine in Judah and Bethlehem. It ends with the harvest. This is a foreshadowing of what is to come in this story. They come home at the barley harvest. This would have been around April and May. Consider all the symbolic resonances that come with spring: a new beginning, a new life, a fresh start, moving out of the dark and death of winter into a new beginning. It is a time of rejoicing. The chapter ends with a ray of hope. The sun is finally breaking through the dark clouds. Naomi may not know what God is doing, but clearly something new is taking place.

3

Boaz, a Second Adam

The way God reverses the fortunes of Naomi and Ruth is a type, or a symbol, of the way he changes the fortunes of Israel. The actions of Boaz in this book, as we will see, are typological of Christ's work as our kinsman-redeemer. Substitute the first Adam for Elimelech, Mahlon, and Chilion. Elimelech misleads his bride in the same way that Adam misled Eve in the Garden. Replace Boaz with Jesus; he is the second Adam, the one who comes and takes the place of the fallen first Adam. Then, put the church in the place of Ruth and Naomi. These two characters merge together in the story and become a composite figure. Now you can see how the book works as a gospel story. The first Adam brought about death. Through the second Adam, through Boaz, there will be restoration and redemption. God will restore Ruth and Naomi to their inheritance, their place in the land, and their stake in the kingdom.

THE KINSMAN-REDEEMER

In verse 1 of Chapter 2, we are introduced to Boaz. We are told he is a relative or kinsman of Naomi's husband. The word that is used is not the word for *kinsman-redeemer* (this word appears later on in the story). At this point, we know he is some kind of relative, but we are not sure if he is a valid candidate to serve as a kinsman-redeemer. It is as though the author wants to tease us with possibilities at the beginning of Chapter 2. And at the end of the chapter, it is revealed that Boaz is a close enough kinsman that he could possibly serve as a kinsman-redeemer.

We are also told of Boaz's great worth. The term has connotations of wealth, might and heroism. We will see how he uses this wealth and status and these privileges on behalf of others, notably Ruth.

Through the introduction of Boaz, the author provides a striking contrast with the weak men who perished in Chapter 1. The name "Boaz" is also found in 1 Kings 7:21: it is the name given to one of the two free-standing pillars in front of Solomon's temple. When Solomon built his temple, he established two great pillars at the front of the temple. One of those pillars was named Boaz, meaning strength. The other pillar was called Jachin, a name which means something like "established." Of course, this was a great honor for Boaz to have one of these pillars in the house of God named after him.

There are several implications to the meaning of Boaz's name. One connection is found in Rev. 3:12. St. John gives us the seven letters to the seven churches. Jesus, writing to the church of Philadelphia, tells them that if they overcome, they will be made pillars in the house of God. That is to say, if they overcome, they will be made Boazes. So, if you want to be a pillar in the house of God, there is no one better to study and imitate than Boaz himself — except of course the foundation upon which the pillars in God's house rest, Jesus Christ himself. If you want to know what kind of materials God uses to build his house, look at Boaz. We will see why that is the case as the story unfolds.

If you turn to the genealogy in Matthew's gospel, you see that Salmon begat Boaz by Rahab and Boaz begat Obed by Ruth, Obed begat Jesse, and Jesse begat David the King. Boaz is in the Messianic line; he points us to the Messiah. What is also worth noting is that Boaz's mother is one of just five women named in the genealogy. It is Rahab, who was herself a foreigner incorporated into Israel by marriage, just as Ruth will be. And if Boaz's mother was a Canaanite, who was grafted into Israel, he would have known something about the plight of a foreigner within the nation of Israel, particularly a foreign woman. This is one reason why he would have been inclined to take special care of Ruth. He would have known something about the plight of strangers and aliens within the commonwealth of Israel. He was aware of how important it was to care for the outcast and the stranger. The Old Testament law greatly emphasized care for the stranger, for the poor, and for widows, and Boaz would have been intimately familiar with these things because his own mother had been in this situation.

In Chapter 2 the story begins to move toward resolution, and God begins to show how he will provide for these two women.

Ruth 2:1-2

> Now Naomi had a relative of her husband's, a worthy man of the clan of Elimelech, whose name was Boaz. And Ruth the Moabite said to Naomi, "Let me go to the field and glean among the ears of grain after him in whose sight I shall find favor." And she said to her, "Go, my daughter."

The text not only refers to Boaz's economic abundance, but to his overall greatness in character and valor. You could even say he's a mighty warrior.

In verse 2, Ruth is seeking to go into the field. The specific field is important and sets a contrast with another detail earlier in the book. When Elimelech leaves Israel, the text says he goes to another field, though most English translations do not capture this nuance. A literal reading of the verse in Chapter 1 reveals that "Elimelech took his family to the field of Moab." The same word appears in Ruth 1:1 and Ruth 1:6, when the word refers to the family returning from the "field" of Moab. When Ruth asks for permission to go into Boaz's field, the text indicates a reversal. Just as Elimelech left God's presence — or God's field — for the field of Moab, so now Ruth has left behind the field of Moab and enters a field in the promised land. The field bears all the worth of the promised land, because it is the field of Boaz.

A Theology of Gleaning

Before continuing this section, it is crucial for the reader to understand what stands behind the Old Testament gleaning laws. In Lev. 19:9-10, we read:

> When you reap the harvest of your land, you shall not wholly reap the corners of your field, nor shall you gather the gleanings of your harvest. You shall not glean your vineyard, nor shall you gather every grape of your vineyard; you shall leave them for the poor and the stranger: I am the LORD your God.

The owner of the field would go through the first time, but leave behind some of his crop. Those gleanings should be left in the field for the poor as well as for the stranger, each of whom could freely pick and eat.

Lev. 23:22 stresses the same idea:

> When you reap the harvest of your land, you shall not wholly reap the corners of your field when you reap, nor shall you gather any gleaning from your harvest. You shall leave them for the poor and for the stranger: I am the LORD your God.

Deut. 24:19-22 offers the basis of the gleaning law:

> When you reap your harvest in your field, and forget a sheaf in the field, you shall not go back to get it; it shall be for the stranger, the fatherless, and the widow that the LORD your God may bless you in all the work of your hands. When you beat your olive trees, you shall not go over the boughs again; it shall be for the stranger, the fatherless, and the widow. When you gather the grapes of your vineyard, you shall not glean it afterward; it shall be for the stranger, the fatherless, and the widow. And you shall remember that you were a slave in the land of Egypt; therefore I command you to do this thing.

God points out Israel's past as slaves and how he cared for them. The Israelites were fatherless, destitute, in the condition of a widow who had no one looking out for them or providing for them, and God redeemed them. Now, in turn, God commands Israel to do the same for others who are in a similar position: You are to imitate my grace toward you by showing this kind of grace and mercy toward others who are in the same kind of situation, those who are enslaved or oppressed in some way.

These gleaning laws are very important because they give us a model of biblical charity. Following are a few additional points concerning this principle.

THE GRACE OF THE GLEANING LAWS

Though the gleaning laws are commanded, they are voluntary. There was no civil punishment, say, for failing to abide by the law. True charity flows out of the heart, not something coerced. Gleaning laws are rooted in relationships, especially in family relationships. This is not a matter of compulsion as in the case of the welfare state where an impersonal bureaucracy gives handouts to people. People are coming into your field and property. This is quite different from using the force of the sword to gather tax money for the purposes of distributing to the poor.

In Matthew 25, Jesus speaks about giving a cup of cold water in his name. Writing a check to the IRS, even if some of that money goes to help the poor, is not the same as giving a cup of cold water to one in need in the name of Christ. This is personal; it is face-to-face and rooted in a relationship that flows out of love.

There is also a wisdom principle here. There is a built-in discriminating factor: the deserving poor are the ones who benefit from help. How? Think about the system of gleaning. There are different kinds of poor people and different reasons why people end up in impoverished conditions. Sometimes it's because they are handicapped, either mentally or physically, and so they simply cannot work and others have to come along and provide for their needs. Certainly, those are people who ought to be objects of our mercy. Other people are poor simply because they are lazy and do not want to work. The gleaning principle helps those who are willing to work. After all, going along in the field to pick up the gleanings or reaping right in the corners of the field would have been hard work. Only those who were able-bodied and then willing to work could have benefited from this system. The gleaning system did nothing to subsidize any kind of laziness, immorality, or greed.

The gleaning system only helped those who were willing to work. This is an important qualification because there is a form of charity that becomes immoral. Scripture speaks of this when it says that even the mercies of the wicked are cruel. There is a way of showing compassion that is actually cruel because it is dehumanizing. That's why the Bible says if you don't work you should not eat; there is a connection between work and eating, between the labor and the fruits of that labor. A person who may not have any money to their name, or any property of their own would be in a very precarious position, but the gleaning laws gave them an opportunity to work and eat. If they were willing to work and go out in the field, to provide for themselves, to work and earn their own living, they would be rewarded.

The two gleaning principles are: 1) it is commanded but voluntary so it is based on love and rooted in relationships. And 2) it is discriminating. It gives to the deserving poor.

Ruth 2:3

> So she set out and went and gleaned in the field after the reapers, and she happened to come to the part of the field belonging to Boaz, who was of the clan of Elimelech.

THE IRONY OF REDEMPTIVE HISTORY

Ruth goes out to glean, and she happens to come upon the part of the field that belongs to Boaz. Again, this is one of those places where English translators have done us a bit of a disservice. The English Standard Version says that "she happened" upon the part of the field that belonged to Boaz. The text actually says something more like "chanced upon," or even, "as luck would have it," she stumbled upon Boaz's field. Of course, God has planned everything, right down to the movement of the sub-atomic particles. There is no *luck* or *chance* in God's world.

The writer uses a literary device to show the reader that this was not Ruth's doing at all; this was not Boaz's doing at all. Humanly speaking this was a chance event, which means this is — beyond any doubt — God's providence that brought this about. It is not humanly orchestrated. Ruth goes out to glean and she finds a long row of fields. Now, many Israelites had no regard for the Jubilee law and probably did not have regard for the gleaning laws either. So, there would have been a lot of fields where she would not have been welcome, where there would have been nothing left to glean, or where she would have been in great danger. She was going to look for a field that was inviting, and she "happened" to come to the part of the field belonging to Boaz.

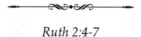

Ruth 2:4-7

> And behold, Boaz came from Bethlehem. And he said to the reapers, "The LORD be with you." And they answered, "The LORD bless you." Then Boaz said to his young man who was in charge of the reapers, "Whose young woman is this?" And the servant who was in charge of the reapers answered, "She is the young Moabite woman, who came back with Naomi from the country of Moab. She said, 'Please let me glean and gather among the sheaves after the reapers.' So she came, and she has continued from early morning until now, except for a short rest."

In verse four, Boaz comes to check on the reapers in his field and uses a formal greeting to hail them. The greeting and response of "The LORD be with you" and "the LORD bless you" should sound familiar to people from liturgical traditions. Western and Eastern liturgies lifted the greeting and response between Boaz and his servants from the book of Ruth and made it a part of their liturgies as a kind of formalized, stylized salutation at the beginning of a service.

The greeting points to Boaz's character. What kind of man greets his servants and workers this way? Boaz is revealing how a godly man treats those who are under his authority. Those of us who are in positions of authority — whether a husband, father or boss — should learn from Boaz how authority ought to be exercised. Boaz's humility points us toward that of another, specifically in Philippians 2, where Jesus, as the God-man, the one who is in the very form of God, does not exploit his God-ness but rather puts it to use in service of his people. Boaz does not use his authority to take advantage of others or to exploit others. Rather,

Boaz uses his power and influence, wealth, and greatness to serve others. We will see that he acts in the same manner with Ruth. He uses all this authority to serve her.

In Ruth 2:5, we find Ruth has already caught Boaz's eye. He asks about her: "Who is this young woman; who does she belong to?" We could read a lot into Boaz's interest, especially in light of the romance of the story. Is this love at first sight? Boaz sees Ruth and immediately wants to know who she is. But something else is going on here.

First of all, remember that gleaning was a highly personalized form of charity. Most likely, Boaz would have known all the gleaners in his field because biblical charity is personal. He would have known the people he was helping. It is natural, therefore, that he would find out about the young woman gleaning in his fields.

Secondly, Boaz notices that Ruth is resting (v. 7). We find out what Ruth had said; this is the report of his chief deputy in the field. She has rested a little in the house. It is clearly emphasized that Ruth has been working very hard. This seems to be what caught Boaz's eye. He wants to know who has come to glean in his field, so there can be contact between the benefactor and the one who is helped. Boaz learns this woman has come back from Moab with Naomi. She asked permission to glean.

KINDNESS SHOWN TO STRANGERS

We've seen the character of Ruth in Chapter 1, but chapter 2 provides further insight. She is a woman and she is a Gentile. In the culture of her time, she already had two strikes against her. And yet, instead of despairing, she sets out to glean, because it is what she needs to do. She knows she is putting herself at risk, considering what all could happen to her in the field. But she trusts God. She doesn't let such obstacles stand in her way. She works hard, and she counts on God to take care of her.

Then Boaz said to Ruth, "Now, listen, my daughter, do not go to glean in another field or leave this one, but keep close to my young women. Let your eyes be on the field that they are reaping, and go after them. Have I not charged the young men not to touch you? And when you are thirsty, go to the vessels and drink what the young men have drawn."

In Ruth 2:8-9, Boaz approaches Ruth and makes it clear that he wants to provide for her welfare. He wants her to stay in his part of the field, and he guarantees her security and protection. It is interesting to see how he addresses her in verse eight. He says, "You will listen, my daughter, will you not? Do not go to glean in another field nor go from here but keep close to my young women." He calls her *daughter*. Some commentators take that as a clue that perhaps there is quite an age difference between Boaz and Ruth, indicating she is a relatively young woman, and he is an older man with a great estate. It is clear that, despite the cost, Boaz intends to provide for Ruth. Boaz is fulfilling his duty to provide for the poor. As it turns out, this is also fulfilling family obligations he would have had since Ruth is a part of his extended family through Naomi, and Ruth has identified herself with Naomi.

Boaz is going beyond what you would ordinarily be required to do. He assures Ruth she can glean without fear of being attacked, which certainly would have been an issue for a woman at that time in that culture. There would have been some danger involved, but he promises her protection. He also gives her the right to glean permanently in his field and tells her to stay with his young women. These young women would have been assistants or attendants in the whole harvest process. So, Ruth is being given special privileges.

Boaz also allows Ruth to have access to their water supply. Of course, this would have been a great blessing from a practical standpoint. Water was very hard to come by for gleaners. This would have prevented her from having to do a lot of tiresome work.

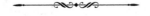

THE LAVISHING GRACE OF BOAZ

Boaz is clearly showering Ruth with grace and protection. He is making promises to her; he is going beyond the ordinary provisions of the law for charity toward people in this situation and even putting her in the same category as his own household servants. In fact, Ruth even acknowledges these benefits in verse 13 when she says that she is not worthy to be one of his maidservants.

Of course, in doing these things, Boaz is a picture of the king and husband Israel needs, one who will protect and provide, one who will freely give food and water to the people under his care. He is doing everything to meet Ruth's needs, showing the kind of man he is. He elevates the status of the lowly and the outcast. He includes the stranger in his own household.

It is important to view this development in light of Elimelech's journey to seek bread in Moab, from the people who previously refused to give bread and water to Israel as they passed through their country. Here, Boaz is the antithesis of Moab.

Ruth 2:10-13

> Then she fell on her face, bowing to the ground, and said to him, "Why have I found favor in your eyes, that you should take notice of me, since I am a foreigner?" But Boaz answered her, "All that you have done for your mother-in-law since the death of your husband has been fully told to me, and how you left your father and mother and your native land and came to a people that you did not know before. The LORD repay you for what you have done, and a full reward be given you by the LORD, the God of Israel, under whose wings you have come to take refuge." Then she said, "I have found favor in your eyes, my lord, for you have comforted me and spoken kindly to your servant, though I am not one of your servants."

How does Ruth respond to this grace? In verse 10, she falls on her face. The text indicates a physical expression of reverence, fear, and gratitude toward Boaz. Then she says, "Why have I found favor in your eyes that you should take notice of me since I am a foreigner?" This is incredible humility on her part. Her question is the question that every Christian puts to God: "Why have I found grace in your sight?" True grace always astonishes the repentant. We know we haven't done anything to earn God's favor. We have done nothing to merit our status. We haven't earned any of the gifts God gives to us. Grace is humbling. Grace is astonishing because we know we do not deserve it. Ruth gives the only proper response to the grace exhibited by another.

The Humility of Ruth

Boaz answers Ruth's question in the same way the Lord answers similar questions from us. Boaz does not say he is extending charity and protection to Ruth because she is physically attractive, which is what we might expect in a Hollywood version of the story. What Boaz says he noticed was her covenant loyalty. The word used to describe her actions is *hesed* — covenant loyalty and devotion. *Hesed*, of course, is a key theme in the book of Ruth. Boaz has noticed that Ruth has been covenantally loyal. This is what makes her so attractive to him.

Ruth is humbled by his show of grace. She is amazed by his grace, you could say. He, in turn, says that Ruth is covenantally loyal, and that is why he is bestowing this grace upon her. Grace upon grace. It is also interesting the precise language he uses here. In verse 11, we read:

> But Boaz answered her, "All that you have done for your mother-in-law since the death of your husband has been fully told to me, and how you left your father and mother and your native land and came to a people that you did not know before."

This language of leaving father and mother, leaving the land of one's birth, and going to a strange land, is a very clear echo of Genesis 12. In Genesis, Abraham is commanded to leave behind the land of his father and mother and go to a strange place, which is the land of promise. Ruth is being put in the place of Abraham. Ruth has the faith of Abraham.

Ruth 2:14

And at mealtime Boaz said to her, "Come here and eat some bread and dip your morsel in the wine." So she sat beside the reapers, and he passed to her roasted grain. And she ate until she was satisfied, and she had some left over.

A Sacramental Table

At mealtime, Boaz invites Ruth to come and eat with them. Like the Gentile woman from Matthew 15, Ruth would likely have been happy just to eat the crumbs falling from the master's table. But in this case, again, as grace is piled upon grace, she is invited to eat at the master's table.

The significance of the ritualization is that the meal is composed of bread and wine. The word that is used here, translated *vinegar*, describes sour wine. In the previous verse, we saw Boaz describe Ruth in Abrahamic terms. Like Abraham, she has left the land of her father and mother to go to this strange place because of God's grace. Boaz feeds her bread and wine, alluding to the meal that Melchizedek served Abraham. Ruth is becoming a new matriarch, a new Sarah. She is fulfilling Abraham's role in this story. Of course, we also could make connections between Genesis 14 and the Lord's Supper. We have taken refuge under the wings of the Lord, and part of that means being fed at his table, just as Ruth is fed at the table of Boaz. We have fellowship with Jesus just as she has fellowship with Boaz here. Also, this puts Boaz himself in the place of Melchizedek. He's a priest-king figure to her. This is the way he is acting on her behalf, and serving her.

To share a meal like this was very significant. This was obviously very hospitable and full of love on the part of Boaz. But it is also a way of saying, "You are a part of my household." This is a highly symbolic and covenantal action. They are having communion at the dinner table together. We've already seen how he includes her among the maid-servants. Now he's going one step further. He is including her in his family. Boaz gives her so much that she is satisfied and even has excess. She has some leftovers she can take home to Naomi.

Again, typologically, this shows us the kind of king that David will be and, of course, ultimately, the kind of king Christ will be. These connections need to be kept in our minds. The first Adam is like Elimelech, like King Saul in the book of Samuel. The first Adam did not provide for the bride. But Boaz, who is a forerunner of David, and ultimately points us to the second Adam, Jesus Christ, provides abundantly for the woman who will become his bride.

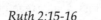

Ruth 2:15-16

> When she rose up to glean, Boaz commanded his young men, saying, "Let her glean even among the sheaves, and do not reproach her. Also, let grain from the bundles fall purposely for her; leave it so that she may glean, and do not rebuke her."

Boaz takes special care to see that Ruth will be successful in gleaning. Ordinarily, all the grain would be bundled up after harvesting, but Boaz wants to make sure that some is left lying around, easy for her to get. As she got food from his table, now she will get grain from his harvest. At this point, Ruth is not even a gleaner anymore. She is no longer an outsider. Boaz has included her in the covenant family; he is giving to her from his supply. Boaz goes far beyond the demands of charity set down in the Torah. He is showing her incredible love and grace.

Ruth 2:17-20

So she gleaned in the field until evening. Then she beat out what she had gleaned, and it was about an ephah of barley. And she took it up and went into the city. Her mother-in-law saw what she had gleaned. She also brought out and gave her what food she had left over after being satisfied. And her mother-in-law said to her, "Where did you glean today? And where have you worked? Blessed be the man who took notice of you." So she told her mother-in-law with whom she had worked and said, "The man's name with whom I worked today is Boaz."And Naomi said to her daughter-in-law, "May he be blessed by the LORD, whose kindness has not forsaken the living or the dead." Naomi also said to her, "The man is a close relative of ours, one of our redeemers."

An ephah is about 36 liters. From the amount of food and grain, Naomi can tell that Ruth received special treatment. Ruth received enough to feed them for several weeks. Ruth gives Naomi the leftover bread from her meal with Boaz. It becomes evident that Boaz is providing from his table and his field for both Ruth and Naomi. Now, Naomi shares in that blessing.

Naomi blesses the man who showered this favor upon Ruth. In Deuteronomy 24, those who show grace toward foreigners are said to be blessed. Ruth identifies this man as Boaz. In fact, verses 19-22 are a chiasm, and right in the middle of that chiasm, is Boaz himself. The text provides an A.-B.-A' structure with Boaz right in the center to show how he acted on behalf of Ruth and Naomi. But ultimately, behind it all, is the Lord's kindness.

Verse 20 is somewhat ambiguous because there is some dispute among translators about the meaning of the phrase, "Whose kindness?" The word for kindness, *hesed*, is used to describe strong covenant loyalty. But whose kindness is in view? Is it the Lord's kindness or is it Boaz's kindness? The answer to this question is it is the Lord's kindness through Boaz. Actually, that reading is made clear in the English Standard Version, which reads: "May he be blessed by the LORD." The translators believe it is a reference to the Lord himself. The Lord has not forsaken his kindness to the living and the dead. But how has the Lord shown this kindness to Ruth and Naomi? He shows kindness by providing Boaz, a priest-king figure who will demonstrate covenant faithfulness and the *hesed* that they need.

Verse 20 is also very different from Naomi's earlier statements. Her statement represents a confession of faith in stark contrast to her earlier complaints in Chapter 1, where Naomi referred to the Lord beating her up. She wouldn't even call him, "Yahweh." She talked about El Shaddai, the Almighty One. Now, she speaks of the Lord's *hesed*. "The Lord is showing me this strong, covenant favor." She has changed her tune because the Lord has wooed her back to himself through providing Boaz. She finds joy in the Lord once again. She has assurance of God's covenant favor toward her. It is safe to conclude that Naomi may have had a temporary lapse of faith or at least a lapse of assurance. But now she has returned. She is no longer bitter. She has been through a death-crisis and now, in a sense, has been resurrected. She is bearing the true faith once again.

THE *GOEL*

Ruth 2:20 concludes by identifying Boaz as a potential kinsman-redeemer. Naomi says to Ruth, "The man is a close relative of ours, one of our redeemers." He is a close kinsman. Actually, the word that's used in the text for "one of our close relations" is *goel*, or kinsman-redeemer.

A kinsman-redeemer was a relative who did for you what you could not do for yourself. He came to your rescue. As a result, he had a whole network of duties and obligations toward the person who was in need. For example, if you were murdered, it was the responsibility of the kinsman-redeemer to track down the slayer and avenge your blood. He would execute vengeance against one who unlawfully took your life. If you were sold into slavery, he would buy you out. The concept of redemption stems from that language.

If you had to sell your inheritance, he would redeem your inheritance for you. If a woman's husband died without leaving her a male heir, the kinsman-redeemer could play the part of the *levir*, but he would act as a substitute husband for her to raise up a male heir and replace the deceased man. Of course, this was because having a son in the Old Covenant was crucial since the whole reason Israel existed was to bring the promised seed of the woman, the son of the covenant, into the world.

Naomi speaks of God's kindness to the living and the dead. How is this kindness to the dead? She is thinking of her deceased husband and sons because in the death of those three back in Chapter 1, their family line and inheritance have been jeopardized. But now, if there's one who can play the part of the levirate and be a levirate husband, then it is also possible a new son to replace Elimelech and Mahlon and Chilion can perhaps be raised up.

Ultimately, all these aspects of the kinsman-redeemer point to Jesus' work for us. The first Adam widowed us and squandered our inheritance and failed to raise up the seed of the woman. He enslaved us to sin. As the second Adam, Jesus produces a fruitful offspring, reclaims our inheritance, rescues us from slavery, and avenges those who seek to murder us. In all these ways, Jesus is our true *levir* and our *goel*, our kinsman-redeemer.

Ruth 2:21

And Ruth the Moabite said, "Besides, he said to me, 'You shall keep close by my young men until they have finished all my harvest.'"

Ruth relays Boaz's special instructions back to Naomi. She is still called Ruth the Moabite. We are being reminded of the fact that she was an outsider who has been brought in. She has been grafted into Israel. Because of her faith and Boaz's grace, she is being made an Israelite.

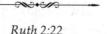

Ruth 2:22

And Naomi said to Ruth, her daughter-in-law, "It is good, my daughter, that you go out with his young women, lest in another field you be assaulted."

Boaz has shown Ruth that he will provide. Naomi's instructions in Ruth 2:22 are not only practical but intended to remind Ruth of the safest and most productive option before her. If Ruth were to think, "I wonder if I am wearing out my welcome, maybe I should go to another part of the field," it would end up insulting Boaz and show that she does not trust him. Again, there is a lesson for us as well. We are to trust in Christ, the greater Boaz, to provide our daily bread. We should not look in other fields, as it were. After all that Christ has done for us, how dare we go elsewhere? We need to keep looking to him; we need to stay in his field working and trusting him.

Ruth 2:23

So she kept close to the young women of Boaz, gleaning until the end of the barley and wheat harvests. And she lived with her mother-in-law.

This verse is a summary statement. Just as Chapter 1 closed out with a summary and then pointed ahead to what was still to come, we find the same thing in the final verse of Chapter 2.

It was harvest time, which was about a two-month period. Some of the issues in this story have been resolved. Remember, there were several problems back in Chapter 1. The basic structure of this book is lack, lack liquidated or need, need met. Some of those needs have already been met. They have been able to eat; they are able to survive. They have a full harvest now to care for their needs.

But there is also something that hasn't been dealt with yet, and the reader can see that issue arise at the end of this passage when it says that "she lived with her mother-in-law." Though Ruth promised to always lodge where Naomi lodged, the statement in the verse reminds the reader that Ruth has not yet been fully incorporated into the household of another man. She still lives with her mother-in-law, which means she is still in need of a husband. She is still in need of a seed to be an heir. So, while some of the issues have been resolved at this point, there is still the question of a husband for Ruth. Of course, at this point it seems clear that Boaz is the one, but how is it going to happen? That's what we're going to see in the chapters to come.

4

A Symbolic Proposal

Ruth 3:1-10

Then Naomi her mother-in-law said to her, "My daughter, should I not seek rest for you, that it may be well with you? Is not Boaz our relative, with whose young women you were? See, he is winnowing barley tonight at the threshing floor. Wash therefore and anoint yourself, and put on your cloak and go down to the threshing floor, but do not make yourself known to the man until he has finished eating and drinking. But when he lies down, observe the place where he lies. Then go and uncover his feet and lie down, and he will tell you what to do." And she replied, "All that you say I will do."So she went down to the threshing floor and did just as her mother-in-law had commanded her. And when Boaz had eaten and drunk, and his heart was merry, he went to lie down at the end of the heap of grain. Then she came softly and uncovered his feet and lay down. At midnight the man was startled and turned over, and behold, a woman lay at his feet. He said, "Who are you?" And she answered, "I am Ruth, your servant. Spread your wings over your servant, for you are a redeemer."

And he said, "May you be blessed by the LORD, my daughter. You have made this last kindness greater than the first in that you have not gone after young men, whether poor or rich."

It's important to remember how Ruth 2 ends. Ruth has been gleaning in the field of Boaz, who has taken special measures to protect her and to provide for and include her, even in his family. When Ruth comes home, Naomi can see how much Ruth has collected. Someone in Bethlehem has shown her great favor. She has returned with more than an ordinary gleaner. The Lord has moved someone to treat her with great kindness. When Naomi finds out it was Boaz, who was a close relative and, therefore, a possible candidate to play the role of a *goel* and of a *levirate*, she starts to develop a plan. By the end of the harvest season, she has devised a strategy for Ruth to stealthily approach Boaz and ask him to act as a kinsman-redeemer.

INDECENT PROPOSAL OR LEGAL APPEAL?

The question that typically arises relates to Ruth going to Boaz in the night. Was this some indecent proposal or is this a legal appeal? The theme of this chapter, as well as the entire book, is seeking security. This is the holistic rest that God promises to his people, which, in this case, would involve a husband to ensure safety, a home, and an heir. Earlier, Naomi wanted rest for Ruth, which is why she tried to send her back to Moab. She said, "Perhaps you will find rest there." The reality is that Naomi wanted a false rest for Ruth. Ultimately, it was an act of unfaithfulness on Naomi's part to even contemplate finding rest in the idolatrous land of Chemosh. Now we find that she is thinking about a godly man like Boaz who could grant rest to Ruth. Again, we must view this development typologically: it is a picture of the rest and security God provides for his people.

What exactly is Naomi telling Ruth to do? In verse 2, Naomi knows Boaz will be working overtime that evening. Apparently, they would take turns at the community threshing floor, and eventually it would be Boaz's turn. As they threshed out the grain, they also would participate in a festival celebration: eating and drinking. The threshing floor, in paganism, was a place of sexual immorality and was tied to the Canaanite religion. In light of some pagan traditions, some commentators try to cast the festival celebration in Ruth in an unfavorable light. But it is important to note that the temple is built on a threshing floor. Because the event in Ruth takes place on a threshing floor, perhaps we have an even stronger reason as to why one of Solomon's great pillars in the temple was named after Boaz. After all, one of Boaz's greatest acts of godliness came on the threshing floor.

A SYMBOLIC PROPOSAL

In Ruth 3:3-4, Naomi tells Ruth to wash and dress as a bride. The actions are: washing, anointing, and dressing. Throughout Scripture, those three actions represent the bride's steps as she prepares to meet her husband. Ruth must go to the place where Boaz is lying down to sleep and uncover his feet. Boaz will understand what to do next.

In verse 5, Ruth pledges to do what Naomi commands. Naomi wants Ruth to go to Boaz and gently remind him that he is a kinsman-redeemer candidate. Thus, he may take Ruth as his bride and raise up a replacement for Elimelech.

One of the strongest arguments that Ruth is acting wickedly is the assumption that the language indicates Ruth is uncovering Boaz's legs. But this does not seem to flow from the logic of the narrative thus far. The whole story points to Boaz as a kinsman-redeemer. And if Ruth is acting immorally, her actions undermine the book's purpose to defend David's kingship and to vindicate David's right to reign. If this was an immoral act, the book of Ruth would have been suppressed rather than published by those who defended David's kingship.

If Ruth is doing something immoral, then Boaz's character is deeply flawed, because he went along with Ruth's proposal. Ruth's act is a symbol of her request. It is a kind of marriage proposal. But it is a special kind of marriage proposal since it is for a levirate marriage. Ruth is petitioning Boaz to act as a kinsman-redeemer on her behalf and, of course, on behalf of Naomi as well.

Again, this is all very odd to us and certainly not to be taken as some kind of model for young women of our time to follow in finding a husband. In Ruth's request that Boaz enter into a levirate marriage, we can see a connection with Tamar. Insofar as Tamar is vindicated, Ruth will be vindicated here as well. The big difference, of course, is that Tamar dressed up as a harlot whereas Ruth dressed up as a bride. The principle in each story is the same.

While Naomi thought Boaz was obviously a good candidate to be the kinsman-redeemer, Boaz is so scrupulously honest and such a faithful man that he is not going to proceed out of order. Boaz is aware of the entire situation, and he knows perhaps something that Naomi did not know, namely, that there is a closer relative. This closer relative must first be given the opportunity to perform these responsibilities toward Ruth.

In Ruth 3:6-7, we see Ruth doing exactly what Naomi has told her to do. Boaz is celebrating with his servants, and then he settles down for a good night's sleep. Ruth comes to him. She uncovers his feet and lies there. In some cases, this language for feet was euphemistic for a man's private parts, but in this case, it is a symbolic gesture. She uncovers his feet and waits for him to wake up. He wakes up startled in the middle of the night and realizes there is a woman present. So he says, "Who are you?" Ruth answers, "I am Ruth, your maidservant." She identifies herself in a humble manner and gives instructions to Boaz. She asks a favor: "Take your maidservant under your wing for you are a kinsman-redeemer." That kinsman-redeemer language clues us into what is taking place. Some commentators assume Ruth is taking matters into her own hands. After all, Naomi's instructions at the beginning of the chapter are for Ruth to do these things, and Boaz will tell her what to do. But here it is Ruth who tells Boaz what to do. The narrator settles this dispute in Ruth 3:6 when it is declared that Ruth does all that her mother-in-law instructs her. In other words, she carries out the plan perfectly, just as Naomi instructed her. Naomi's instructions, as detailed in the passage, are not comprehensive, but Ruth went in full knowledge of the request she was making.

The language in Ruth 3:9 is crucial. It is important to remember that Ruth's request to Boaz echoes Boaz's prayer to the Lord in Ruth 2. Ruth is giving Boaz an opportunity to answer his own prayer. Boaz had prayed for her well-being, and now he is going to have an opportunity to fulfill that prayer himself.

The Encounter and a Marriage Proposal

Ruth asks Boaz to spread his wings over her. This is a request for a levirate marriage. This is marital language indicating they would be bound together. They are now bound together by this one cloth. Sharing one garment is a sign of a husband and wife becoming one flesh. Ruth is inviting him to perform these levirate responsibilities, which include marriage.[9]

The Legal Basis of Ruth's Request

Is the request that Ruth makes—this marriage invitation— out of order? This is not a typical process, but there is a legal basis for the request, found in the levirate institution and the *goel* institution. She is acting according to biblical principles that were enforced at her time. She has a right to make the request, because the levirate and *goel* institutions are at work. She is simply asking Boaz to do what the law would have called him to do. She is not, as some have suggested, repeating the sin of the Moabite women: when the Israelite men came out of slavery in Egypt, the Moabite women went and seduced them into sexual sin. That is not the case in Ruth. In fact, if anything, Ruth's request is a reversal of

---

9   A lengthy introduction to the theology of wings is found in Appendix B. The reader may wish to read that essay before continuing.

the story of the Israelite men committing sexual immorality with Moabite women. What Ruth does is obviously virtuous, and Boaz calls attention to that aspect of her actions in Ruth 3:10-13:

> And he said, "May you be blessed by the LORD, my daughter. You have made this last kindness greater than the first in that you have not gone after young men, whether poor or rich. [11] And now, my daughter, do not fear. I will do for you all that you ask, for all my fellow townsmen know that you are a worthy woman. [12] And now it is true that I am a redeemer. Yet there is a redeemer nearer than I. [13] Remain tonight, and in the morning, if he will redeem you, good; let him do it. But if he is not willing to redeem you, then, as the LORD lives, I will redeem you. Lie down until the morning."

Boaz properly understood Ruth's request. We have already been introduced to Boaz as a great and God-fearing man. He does not wake up with this woman at his feet and say, "Get away from me." He understands the symbolic act because, like Naomi, and now like Ruth, he knows the law of God and the responsibilities that would fall to a close relative. In fact, that is why he identifies Ruth's act as an act of *hesed*. This whole scene is not about *eros*, but about *hesed*. The focus of the story is on covenant faithfulness and covenant kindness.

Boaz says that this is a greater act of kindness than her first act of kindness. The first act of kindness was coming back with Naomi to Judah from the land of Moab, leaving her homeland and false gods behind to become a part of the people of Israel with Naomi. But now this second act of kindness is even greater. Boaz understands that this is a proposal for a kinsman-redeemer marriage. He knows that Ruth could have sought out a spouse of her choosing. She could have sought out a man closer to her age. Instead, she sought to marry Boaz because then, and only then, as far as she knows, would there be a levirate marriage in which a child could be raised up to inherit Naomi's property and preserve Elimelech's name. Naomi needs a new Adam; Ruth asks Boaz to be this new Adam. She is acting not in her own interests, but on behalf of Naomi. Whatever romantic aspect is built into this, it is primarily about Ruth acting on Naomi's behalf to secure an heir.

Also, Boaz acknowledges that Ruth was not obligated to seek a levirate marriage. According to the levirate institution, if there was another brother in the home, there would have been obligation there. But because Elimelech had no brothers, and there were no other sons in the family for Ruth to marry, she does not have to enter into a levirate marriage. She could make herself available to other men in the community. But, again, because she is acting in *hesed* and has bound herself to Naomi, she is going to marry within the family so that that first male child raised up will be the one who takes Elimelech's place. Of course, all this is in accordance with the oath she took in Ruth 1.

Ruth 3:11-12

> "...And now, my daughter, do not fear. I will do for you all that you ask, for all my fellow townsmen know that you are a worthy woman. And now it is true that I am a redeemer. Yet there is a redeemer nearer than I."

A CLOSER REDEEMER

In verses 11 and 12, Boaz pledges to do what Ruth has requested and praises her virtue. Ruth's excellence and her great virtue are well known in the community. The language used to praise Ruth is the same type of language found in Proverbs 31, in which Solomon praises the virtuous wife. Boaz delivers similar praise for Ruth. But there is a plot twist. Everything seems to be proceeding according to plan, and now things take a sharp turn. A wrench is thrown into Naomi's plan. In verse 12, we find out there is a closer relative than Boaz, one who has the first right of taking up the honorable role of *goel*. This is part of what makes Ruth such a beautiful story. The way the story is crafted at every turn creates suspense and introduces several surprises.

The fact that there is a closer redeemer explains other details in the story. The existence of a closer relative would explain why Boaz had not already acted on his own initiative to pursue Ruth's hand in marriage. Naomi and Ruth might be wondering why Boaz has not acted to set things in motion himself. Why does the initiative have to fall to Ruth? Boaz is an honorable man; he is not going to act out of line. Boaz is going to wait and see what the other man, the closer relative, does. Boaz might desperately want to marry Ruth, but he restrains himself because, according to the law of God, there is an order to be followed.

We might also ask whether Naomi knew about the closer relative. Boaz is identified as a close relative, but Naomi may have lost track of family records during all the years she was in Moab. It is obvious when she first comes back that she is not altogether aware of Boaz. So it is likely she does not know about this closer relative. We should also note that if Boaz had been the closest relative, he could have consummated the marriage that very night. That is what Ruth is asking him to do. When she comes and sits at his feet and proposes marriage, there is no need for a long betrothal period or a big wedding ceremony. The marriage could be consummated there, privately. This helps us make sense of Ruth's actions.

When Ruth comes to him, she's asking him to marry her that night and to consummate the marriage. Boaz is not prepared to do so because there is a closer relative who gets to step in line first. It is clear that Boaz wants to redeem Ruth, but obeying the law is even more important to him. He practices self-discipline. He puts obedience above his romantic interests.

Ruth 3:13

"...Remain tonight, and in the morning, if he will redeem you, good; let him do it. But if he is not willing to redeem you, then, as the LORD lives, I will redeem you. Lie down until the morning."

What do we see next? In verse 13, Boaz promises to act on Ruth's behalf. He will see to it that the *goel* duty is fulfilled. He promises to defer to the closer relative. If the closer relative acts, Ruth will be taken care of, and she will end up with a closer relative who will bring her into the rest, which Naomi spoke of at the beginning of the chapter. Things will be restored but through this other man. Though there is an expectation of hope that Boaz will marry Ruth, she receives assurance that one way or another she will be provided security. Boaz is a true and a clear picture of godly masculinity. When the opportunity comes to him, Boaz eagerly and aggressively seeks to fulfill his responsibilities. He sets out to do what needs to be done, and he makes promises that he will get it done.

From a literary standpoint, one of the most interesting things about this aspect of the story is that we are not told anything about the emotions of Ruth and Boaz at this point. If a modern writer wrote the story of Ruth, it would probably go on for pages talking about every little detail of their feelings. It is not that those details are unnecessary; they certainly have a place. But the Bible rarely tells us what its characters are thinking and feeling. If ever there was a time we would want to know, it would be here.

But the Bible leaves such details to our sanctified imagination. These are gaps in the story that our imaginations are free to fill. Also, the storyteller does not want us to focus on the romance, although it is a subtext to the story. It is not explicit, but you can detect some hints that Boaz and Ruth like each other. But the book of Ruth is about *hesed*. Righteousness in the Bible satisfies covenant obligations. When Boaz speaks of Ruth's virtue, this is what he has in mind. She is virtuous because she satisfies her relational obligations. Her obligations in this case are to Naomi, and so she is going to see to it that she acts on Naomi's behalf. Boaz, in turn, is going to act on her behalf (and on behalf of Naomi as well) to see to it that they find the security they need. Though there are romantic overtones, covenant loyalty is central to the book of Ruth.

Ruth 3:14-15

So she lay at his feet until the morning, but arose before one could recognize another. And he said, "Let it not be known that the woman came to the threshing floor." And he said, "Bring the garment you are wearing and hold it out." So she held it, and he measured out six measures of barley and put it on her. Then she went into the city.

In verse 14, Boaz sends Ruth back to Naomi early in the morning to protect her integrity and reputation. He does not want to give the town gossips anything to talk about. They have done nothing wrong, but Boaz wants to be careful to avoid the appearance of evil.

NIGHT AND DAY IN RUTH

The time at which the book of Ruth's decisive point happens directs our attention to an interesting biblical theme pertaining to all redemptive history. We have already seen how the book is a two-Adam story. The first Adam (Elimelech and his two sons) go on a self-imposed exile from the Promised Land. They are cursed and die, leaving the bride stranded. The second Adam (Boaz) arrives as the kinsman-redeemer.

With that typology in mind, the book of Ruth's turning point takes place at night. In fact, we are told it is the middle of the night. The bride is chosen in the night time.

But as the story unfolds, we will see the marriage is not consummated until day time. The text clearly calls attention to the timing of the events.

The text reveals a progression. In verse 2, we are told that it is night time. In verse 8, we are told that it is midnight, and verse 13 mentions — twice — that it is morning. In verse 18, Naomi directly refers to the day time, specifically the light time of the day, as the time when the matter would be settled.

The entire Old Covenant period happens at night time. This is when God is preparing his people for redemption. The bride, Israel, is chosen during this time, but the marriage itself does not take place until after the break of day. When does daylight break? The coming of Jesus is the dawning of a new day and the beginning of the light time in history. When Jesus comes, he's the light of the world. Now the sun is rising, according to Malachi's prophecy. John 1 speaks of the light now entering the world. The Old Covenant has been a period of darkness.

We can see this motif in John 3 where Nicodemus, a great Old Covenant teacher, comes to Jesus at night because he's still in the dark. He represents the Old Covenant Jews who cannot comprehend the light that has now come. And Jesus speaks of this new birth, pointing Nicodemus to a new era in history that is about to dawn, the regeneration of all things when the light will break. This is why the days in Genesis 1 proceed from darkness to light. The movement is from darkness to light, not only at the beginning when everything is dark and God adds light. But the day itself is structured in terms of a dark period and then a light period. That's how the days run, because it is a symbol of redemptive history, moving from dark to light. Paul speaks of this in Rom. 13:12 when he refers to the night being far spent. He's talking about the Old Covenant winding down. The day is about to break, the new age is about to come in its fullness, and the sun is rising on the world.

In Ruth 3, salvation, or redemption, is contracted at night, and it is fulfilled in the daytime. That is a symbol, or picture, of redemptive history. The promise of redemption is made in the night time; it is fulfilled in the daytime. That is the structure of redemptive history, moving from darkness to light, from promise to fulfillment, from evening to morning, from night time to day time.

For example, we could look back at the Passover. It is in the middle of the night when the angel of death passes them by. The exodus happens the next day. The crossing of the Red Sea represents Israel's baptismal marriage into union with Moses as God's representative. The same kind of structure is found at the cross. It is not night time on the calendar, but he makes it night because he makes it dark. Then, of course, the resurrection happens at daybreak. So there is a midnight event and a daybreak event. At the break of day, Jesus meets Mary Magdalene, a woman. In a sense, that meeting represents the marriage to his church. Just as Adam slept and awoke to meet his bride, so Jesus sleeps on the cross and in the tomb and awakes on the third day to meet the bride. In this manner, Boaz sleeps through the night with Ruth at his feet and the next day he will meet his bride, and everything will be accomplished.

———— ❧✦☙ ————

SIGNS AND SEALS OF THE PROMISE

In Ruth 3:15, Boaz gives Ruth a token. He performs a symbolic gesture to embody his promise to find her a redeemer, even if it is ultimately himself. He gives her not just words, but a sign. This is how God works with his people, and it is how Boaz works with Ruth. This is a sign that will give her even greater confidence, sealing his promise of her redemption.

As a token, Boaz gives Ruth six ephahs of barley. The word "ephahs" is italicized, which means it is not part of the Hebrew text. Translators added the word to help the sentence make sense to English readers. Literally, it reads: "Bring the shawl that is on you and hold it, and when she held it he measured six of barley and laid it on her and then she went into the city." The writer wants to draw attention to the number six.

In verse 17, Ruth points out there are six ephahs of barley, but again, the word "ephahs" is not there. Why six? The six guarantees there will be a seventh. If Boaz gave six, surely he will give seven. He will complete what he began. The number six represents the status of the situation and hints at its possible outcome.

Ruth's Sabbath Rest

It is difficult to take in all the literary artistry present in the text. At the beginning of the chapter, Naomi encourages Ruth to seek rest. The word is translated "security," but she actually says "rest." The chapter ends with Boaz giving "six" to Ruth. It is Boaz's way of showing Ruth he will provide rest.

In fact, in Ruth 3:18, the word for "rest" is repeated. Naomi says, "Wait, my daughter until you learn how the matter turns out, for the man will not rest but will settle the matter today." Ruth can rest, because Boaz will not rest until the matter is settled.

The whole chapter hinges on seeking rest for Ruth, first with Naomi and then Boaz. The six symbolically anticipates the seventh. Just as the night anticipates the day, so the six anticipates the coming seventh ephah — the Sabbath rest for Ruth. The story will not be complete until Ruth enters into this holistic rest, when she's given a husband as well as a son and heir, and a home among the people of God. All those lacks that we encountered at the beginning of the story will finally be liquidated. All those needs will finally be met. Everything that had been lost will be restored and then some. We will have come full circle and the covenant curses will have been turned into covenant blessings. The six ephahs of barley points to the fact that the period of waiting is almost over. In a sense, we could say the night is far spent, the day is at hand. The six are here, the seventh, the Sabbath rest is about to come.

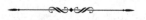

Ruth 3:16-18

> And when she came to her mother-in-law, she said, "How did you fare, my daughter?" Then she told her all that the man had done for her, saying, "These six measures of barley he gave to me, for he said to me, 'You must not go back empty-handed to your mother-in-law.'" She replied, "Wait, my daughter, until you learn how the matter turns out, for the man will not rest but will settle the matter today."

The real meaning of the question in verse 16 is lost on us. Instead of "How did you fare my daughter?" the question is more accurately translated as "Who are you, my daughter?" You went out as Ruth, a single woman; are you returning as the beloved of Boaz? Naomi expected the marriage to be consummated that night. If he was the closest redeemer and she goes to him, he is either going to perform this duty or not. If he does, it would be consummated, and she would become his wife right there on the threshing floor. That is what Naomi was expecting to happen, so when Ruth comes back, she says, "Who are you? Who are you coming back as? Are you now the wife of Boaz?"

In verse 17, Ruth explains, "These six measures of barley he gave to me, for he said to me, 'You must not go back empty-handed to your mother-in-law.'" This balances out Ruth 1, verse 21, in which Naomi complained that she went out full and the Lord has brought her home again empty. She came home empty-handed; now her hands are full — six handfuls in fact, of barley, have been given to her. The emptiness has been reversed. There is a transition from wrath to grace, from curse to blessing. This is a U-shaped story. You begin with Elimelech and his family living in Bethlehem; they go into Moab where they face curse and death. But then they come out on the other side, and Naomi and Ruth are redeemed by Boaz, and everything is restored, even super-restored, you could say. This is a comedy, not a tragedy. Comedies,

66

in the classic sense, are not just stories that make us laugh; they are
stories that turn out well, that have a happy ending, so to speak.
And certainly, the book of Ruth is such a comedy.

As Christians, we can say that comedies reveal the gospel. The
gospel itself is the ultimate comedy/drama, and other stories that
fit the pattern are copies of the gospel in some way. Ruth's story
is the gospel story. God enters into a world full of pain, suffering,
emptiness, death, loneliness, and despair. And he provides rest,
security, life, and joy through a redeemer, a second Adam figure
that comes and reverses the curse. Ruth's story is our story. It is
the church's story. This story is our story if we have been grafted
into Christ, who is the greater Boaz and the ultimate *goel*, the final
levirate husband.

THE SYMBOLISM OF RUTH

One other note concerning the symbolism of the story: Boaz
makes his promise to Ruth, but then he goes off on his own. Ruth
will not be there when he acts decisively to redeem her in the
next chapter. That pattern should point the reader, in a shadowy,
symbolic way to what Jesus does. Think about Jesus when he
finally goes to accomplish redemption. The disciples scatter. They
are not there. He goes through it alone. In a sense, the disciples
rest. They get to fall back and sleep. You can even think of Jesus
with the disciples in the garden before he goes to the cross. They
are resting while he is working. He works redemption while they
rest. In the same way, Boaz is going to go and complete Ruth's
redemption while she rests. Naomi says to Ruth, "You rest, he is
going to go take care of the matter. He is going to work out your
redemption for you, totally apart from you, alone." Again, this
points us to Jesus as our sole redeemer.

Sometimes it is easy to read biblical narratives as though they
were like Aesop's Fables. Then you get to the end and say, "Okay,
what was the moral of the story?" There are all kinds of moral

lessons in the book of Ruth, no doubt, but the most important feature in the story is to see the way God brings salvation to his people and brings them into the promised rest.

If anything, a story such as Ruth shows us that God is the one who acts to rescue us. This is a story about what God does for you, not what you do for God.

5

A Name Remembered

The entire story in the book of Ruth took place during that chaotic, rebellious period of Israel's history. The period of the Judges ends with these words, "There was no king in Israel." The truth, however, is that Israel does have a King — Yahweh is King in Israel. But because no one acknowledges his kingship, there is no king in Israel and thus, as it says at the end of the book of Judges, "Every man does what is right in his own eyes." Elimelech does what is right in his own eyes at the beginning of Ruth. It is ironic that his name means "God is King," because he does not act like it.

The book of Ruth is the answer to Israel's kingship dilemma. God will provide a king for the people. He will provide a king after his own heart, a lion of the tribe of Judah who will lead the people in righteousness. And David, the last word in the book of Ruth, will be that king, in contrast to the end of the book of Judges. The book acts as a bridge from the period of the patriarchs and the judges into this new monarchical phase of God's history in which they will have a king.

As we turn to Ruth 4, we must also keep in mind the events at the end of Ruth 3. There is certainty that Ruth will be redeemed, but there is uncertainty as to whether that redemption will include Boaz, who, from all indications, would like to grant this rest to Ruth himself by marrying her and by raising up a seed for Naomi to be Elimelech's replacement. But Ruth 3 reveals there is an obstacle in the form of a closer kinsman who will get first shot at playing the role of *goel*. One part of this story has been resolved: Ruth will be married.

But there is another aspect of the story that is unresolved, and that is the identity of the kinsman-redeemer. The narrator sets up the drama so that everyone in the audience is hoping for a marriage between Ruth and Boaz. The closer relative becomes a threat to the happy ending of the story we all want to see. So what is going to happen? Will the closer kinsman marry Ruth, or will he pass up the honor and allow Boaz to do it? That's the question, as we enter Ruth 4.

Ruth 4:1

Now Boaz had gone up to the gate and sat down there. And behold, the redeemer, of whom Boaz had spoken, came by. So Boaz said, "Turn aside, friend; sit down here." And he turned aside and sat down.

The city gate was not only the entry and exit point of the city, but it was the place where elders gathered to pass judgments (cf. Prov. 31:23).

Ruth 4:2

And he took ten men of the elders of the city and said, "Sit down here." So they sat down.

Boaz gathers together ten men to form a court. According to Jewish tradition, it takes ten men to form an official court. These men will sit and judge the matter. This is the origin of the word "session." It means to sit in judgment or sit in rule, and that is what they are going to do.

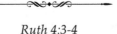

Ruth 4:3-4

> Then he said to the redeemer, "Naomi, who has come back from the country of Moab, is selling the parcel of land that belonged to our relative Elimelech. So I thought I would tell you of it and say, 'Buy it in the presence of those sitting here and in the presence of the elders of my people.' If you will redeem it, redeem it. But if you will not, tell me, that I may know, for there is no one besides you to redeem it, and I come after you." And he said, "I will redeem it."

Boaz summarizes the situation. Naomi has had to sell Elimelech's share of the land. This is a detail that the narrator has suppressed until now, but it suddenly becomes essential. The Israelites were not to sell their God-given plots of land (cf. Lev. 25). If they had to do so, the land should be redeemed (bought back) as soon as possible. If that did not happen, it would revert back to the original family in the Jubilee year (every fiftieth year). But it was much better to get the family land back before that. Ideally, if the land was to be sold, say, out of economic necessity, a kinsman-redeemer would arise and redeem it immediately.

The closer kinsman says he will redeem this parcel of land. Of course, this is where the whole audience is supposed to let out this sigh and say, "Oh, no, this is terrible." The closer relative's reasoning was likely something like this: Naomi is an old woman by now, and there is no possibility of her having children, which is something Naomi admitted in Ruth 1. There will not be an heir of Elimelech to grow up and take the land back into his family, so this closer relative thinks he has an opportunity to increase his own family's holdings. He can increase his share and inheritance in the Promised Land, and he can do so at a relatively low cost. It looks like Boaz will be shut out of the kinsman-redeemer role and will not get to marry Ruth after all.

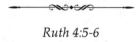

Ruth 4:5-6

> Then Boaz said, "The day you buy the field from the hand of Naomi, you also acquire Ruth the Moabite, the widow of the dead, in order to perpetuate the name of the dead in his inheritance." Then the redeemer said, "I cannot redeem it for myself, lest I impair my own inheritance. Take my right of redemption yourself, for I cannot redeem it."

BOAZ'S STRATEGY

In spite of the closer relative's declaration he will redeem the land, Boaz does not flinch; his plan is much like Naomi's plan in the previous chapter. In verse 5, Boaz plays his trump card, his ace in the hole. You can see that Boaz wants to obey the law; that is why he told Ruth that night on the threshing floor that he must first consult the closer redeemer, but Boaz also wants to marry Ruth. If he can obey the law and get Ruth as well, that would be the best situation of all.

In verse 5, Boaz adds that Ruth comes with Elimelech's property. There is a woman of marriageable age who will raise up a seed to replace Elimelech. Clearly, then, when the seed is old enough, he will take over Elimelech's property once again and it will be his inheritance. The closer kinsman will have to pay for the land while the son grows up, but he will not be able to keep it in his family and pass it on to his own sons. Rather, it will revert to the son he has with Ruth. This means he will have the additional cost of caring not only for Naomi, but also for Ruth, and the children that she has. Suddenly, what looked like a great deal now begins to look like an economic liability. So the closer relative performs a quick recalculation and decides this is not such a good investment after all. And in verse 6, the closer relative says he cannot do it because it would be too expensive in the long run. Much to Boaz's pleasure, the closer kinsman passes up Ruth and Naomi's estate; he waives his right of redemption.

We might ask, "Why did Boaz present this deal in two stages, saving the marriage part, the part where the man would have to marry Ruth, until the end?" It seems the narrator wants us to see this as a very shrewd act on Boaz's part. It is somewhat difficult to articulate Boaz's strategy. We would probably need to have been there to see the genius of it. But perhaps if he had presented both the land acquisition and Ruth all at once, then the man would not have been so careful to consider what marriage to Ruth would have cost him. Or, perhaps separating Ruth allowed Boaz to call special attention to her nationality, making the prospect of marriage to her rather unattractive to this man. Whatever the case, the scene clearly shows that Boaz is both clever and wise — and perhaps in love with a Moabite.

The Nameless Relative

Before moving on, there is another detail to consider in the passage. We have already seen how important names are throughout the book of Ruth, particularly in how they reveal character. But the closer kinsman is not named at all. He is an unnamed kinsman. Why is he not given a name? Everybody else in the story has a name. When the Holy Spirit gives a character a name, that name has significance. When the Holy Spirit withholds a name, that fact is important, as well.

The author probably concealed the identity of this man so as not to embarrass his family or his descendants living at the time of writing. While the book is establishing Boaz and his family, there is no reason to tear down this other man. Concerning the developments in the story, the closer kinsman is nameless because his name is not worth mentioning. He has refused to perpetuate his brother's name in Israel, and so his name will not be perpetuated in the story.

There is a kind of *lex talionis* (a law of retaliation) in the narrative. He did not build up his brother's house and carry on his brother's name, so his name will not be carried on. He does not become a *goel*, because he fears it would jeopardize his inheritance and name. As a result, his name is lost. He missed his chance to make his name great in Israel. The man appears to be concerned only with money. He views the redemption of another as too costly. The lesson from this man's example would be something like this: Do not let greed keep you from helping needy, covenant members. If you allow your greed to get in the way of helping those in the covenant who are in need, you are in danger of having God blot your name out. You will become nameless and forgotten. The way to have your name remembered and perpetuated by the covenant people is to become a generous person, to be a redeemer of people who are in need. The closer kinsman turns out to be a false redeemer.

Ruth 4:7-8

> Now this was the custom in former times in Israel concerning redeeming and exchanging: to confirm a transaction, the one drew off his sandal and gave it to the other, and this was the manner of attesting in Israel. So when the redeemer said to Boaz, "Buy it for yourself," he drew off his sandal.

In verses 7 and 8, we are introduced to the custom of sandal exchange. Earlier, we referred to a similar practice in Deuteronomy 25 where the brother who refuses to be a *levir* has his feet uncovered and gets spit in his face. The custom looks a bit different here. Was this a valid transformation of that tradition described in Deuteronomy 25? It appears that the custom is different, but it is also very clearly related. Perhaps it is a little different because the degree of shame was not as great in the case of this man as it would have been in the case of the man in Deuteronomy 25 who refuses to perform the levirate duty altogether. The closer relative in Ruth 4 probably does not have to be a levirate because there is some distance in familial relation, and also there is another candidate who can do it and is willing to do so. Hence, the closer relative is not entirely abandoning the situation. He sees to it that something is done for Ruth and Naomi, but he does not do it himself. There is a degree of shame, but a lesser degree of shame. This may explain why there is no spitting in the face as the custom required. There is perhaps some public humiliation involved, but it is not as full as what it would have been in the situation that the text in Deuteronomy envisions.

The sandal exchange custom also is a way to ratify transactions; it is probably the way that ancient Israelites sealed legal deals. The shoe business in front of the elders was probably a lot like our use of a notary public to ratify an official document, especially since the particular transaction in Ruth 4 involves land and marriage. The exchange of the shoe probably implies that one man will walk in the other's shoes in this matter. The one man will stand in the place of the other and fulfill his obligations.

Ruth 4:9-10

> Then Boaz said to the elders and all the people, "You are witnesses this day that I have bought from the hand of Naomi all that belonged to Elimelech and all that belonged to Chilion and to Mahlon. Also Ruth the Moabite, the widow of Mahlon, I have bought to be my wife, to perpetuate the name of the dead in his inheritance, that the name of the dead may not be cut off from among his brothers and from the gate of his native place. You are witnesses this day."

In a largely oral culture in which most people could not learn to read and write, people would hear Boaz's declaration officially proclaimed and it would live in their collective memory. There are multiple witnesses present to attest to the deal. As Boaz takes possession of the land, he also takes Ruth for his wife in a levirate marriage.

The transaction is sealed. He has taken possession of the land, and he has taken possession of Ruth as his wife. Again, as mentioned previously, there is no need in this particular case for a betrothal period or ceremony. Apparently, she would immediately become his wife because this is a levirate marriage. He is taking over the marriage of another. Of course, this marriage will include the raising up of a seed for Elimelech to inherit his land and to carry on his name.

Ruth 4:11-12

> Then all the people who were at the gate and the elders said, "We are witnesses. May the LORD make the woman, who is coming into your house, like Rachel and Leah, who together built up the house of Israel. May you act worthily in Ephrathah and be renowned in Bethlehem, and may your house be like the house of Perez, whom Tamar bore to Judah, because of the offspring that the LORD will give you by this young woman."

The elders affirm all the purposes of Boaz's actions. They put their seal of approval on the transaction as witnesses, so this has been ratified. We also have the twin blessings that are given in the closing verses, one from the elders and another from the women of the city. The connections they make with earlier figures in Israel's history are necessary. They help shed light on various aspects of this story.

The elders give a three-fold blessing: The first of these is, "May Ruth be like Rachel and Leah who built up the house of Israel by raising up godly seed and perpetuating the covenant line with many children." Ruth is connected with the matriarchs of Israel.

Secondly, "May you prosper in Ephrathah and be famous in Bethlehem." Indeed Boaz did become famous, not just in Bethlehem but all of Israel. Not only through this book but also through one of the great pillars in Solomon's temple that bore his name. Further, he becomes a member of the messianic line and is recorded in the New Testament genealogies of Jesus Christ.

The third blessing is, "May your house be like the house of Perez whom Tamar bore to Judah." This third benediction links the entire story with Genesis 38 and the levirate marriage concept, which was at work in that story.

The Role of Tamar in Ruth's Gospel

There are several things to note in light of the connection with Genesis 38. Ruth is a new Tamar. While Tamar dressed up as a prostitute and deceived Judah, Ruth dressed up like a bride and approached Boaz, but each woman is taking action for the same reasons. Their ultimate concern is for the covenant line. Though their actions may seem immoral, the actions should not be viewed that way within the framework of biblical law. Judah condemns himself and vindicates Tamar after he realizes what has happened. And the way that the book of Ruth plays out vindicates Ruth from any wrongdoing. She went to Boaz because, in her and Naomi's understanding, he was the closest relative. He was the prime candidate to be the kinsman-redeemer.

Obviously, we cannot say the actions of Tamar and Ruth serve as patterns for today's Christian women or young women seeking husbands. But Tamar and Ruth acted because of their concerns for the covenant promise and the seed line, and that is exemplary. For that reason, they serve as models for us. Judah is the chosen tribe and, if the seed of the woman promised in Gen. 3:15 is going to come into the world, the line must be perpetuated. The reader should be grateful for what these women did, because without them there would have been no Advent and no redemption. It is through these women that the line leads to Jesus. In 1 Tim. 2:15, Paul says women are saved in childbearing. These women are saved in childbearing, not only in the sense of being rescued from difficult situations in life, but also because they are taking part in redemptive history. In the book of Ruth, the woman plays her role by perpetuating the seed, ultimately culminating with Mary, who brings the promised seed into the world.

It is worth reiterating that Tamar and Ruth were each widows seeking levirate marriages. Each woman was a Gentile who was grafted into the covenant through a levirate marriage. Not only does Ruth's actions recall Tamar, but Boaz also is compared to Perez: "May Boaz's house be like Perez's house." Why Perez? Perez's house was much larger than the house of his brother, Zerah. In fact, Perez's house was so large it eventually had to be split. In Numbers 26, we learn that Perez is so fruitful his descendants have to be divided into two distinct families, recalling God's promise to Abraham and the blessing God gave to Rebekah in Genesis 24: the expansiveness of their households. In this manner, the benedictions in the book of Ruth point to the growth and fullness of the kingdom of God.

Ruth 4:13

> So Boaz took Ruth, and she became his wife. And he went in to her, and the LORD gave her conception, and she bore a son.

We find that the marriage of Ruth and Boaz did, in fact, produce a son. This child was a gift of the Lord, as all children are. Conception, in Scripture, is always due to the Lord's action. The wording in verse 13 makes this point. It is not Boaz, but the Lord who ultimately causes her to conceive. It is important to remember that Ruth was previously married but had not conceived a son. The fact that the text mentions the Lord giving her conception suggests Ruth would have been barren apart from some special intervention of the Lord. Like all the other matriarchs in the book of Genesis who are barren until God intervened and opened their wombs, so it is with Ruth. The Lord acts through Boaz the way he acted through Abraham. He does for Ruth what he did for Sarah. These are connections we must make. She had already been married for ten years, so it is safe to assume she was barren. But here the Lord acts on her behalf.

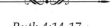

Ruth 4:14-17

> Then the women said to Naomi, "Blessed be the LORD, who has not left you this day without a redeemer, and may his name be renowned in Israel. He shall be to you a restorer of life and a nourisher of your old age, for your daughter-in-law who loves you, who is more to you than seven sons, has given birth to him." Then Naomi took the child and laid him on her lap and became his nurse. And the women of the neighborhood gave him a name, saying, "A son has been born to Naomi." They named him Obed. He was the father of Jesse, the father of David.

Notice that this blessing is directed to Naomi, not to Boaz or to Ruth. Why is this? Because it serves to reverse the speech of Naomi to the women back in Ruth 1:20-21. Now every problem experienced by Naomi at the story's beginning has been solved and now they call her blessed. God has restored her.

6

A Doxological Ending

As we come to the end of the book, the women of the city praise the Lord (Ruth 4:14). God gets credit for all the good things that have happened. God has brought about a series of surprising reversals. He has brought Naomi from emptiness to fullness. Naomi was blaming the Lord, but now God receives glory for restoring her. She was a widow, but now she has a man who will protect and provide for her. She was childless, but now a child has been raised up to take the place of her fallen sons. She was in danger of starvation, but now she enjoys the abundance and prosperity of Boaz's house. God has provided a holistic rest and salvation for Naomi and Ruth. This is fitting, for the gospel is a message of reversal. The gospel is a message of God bringing life out of death, acquittal out of guilt, righteousness out of unrighteousness. The gospel is a message of reversal as the second Adam undoes the curse of the first Adam.

The son born to Ruth and Boaz is said to be a *goel*, a kinsman-redeemer. Consider the language of Ruth 4:15: "May he be to you a restorer of life." The language indicates a kinsman-redeemer, and if the son is said to be a *goel*, the question becomes: Who is the real kinsman-redeemer? Is it Boaz or is it the son that is born, Obed? The answer is both. Each in his own way foreshadows Jesus Christ.

Such an answer may point to some people's frustration with biblicaly typology: How can different people fulfill the same role in the same story? It's because Jesus is so multi-faceted and so full that one person is not enough to symbolize him. Just as the church in this story is symbolized by Naomi and Ruth together, so Jesus Christ is symbolized by Boaz, as well as Obed. Christ is both husband and son. He is both Boaz and Obed. He is the seed of the woman. He is the child of the promise, who, like Isaac, is sacrificed. But he is also the husband who marries the widowed people as a second Adam and who makes the people, the Bride, fruitful. All those things are at work in these closing verses. In the typology of Ruth, marriage and birth are conflated.

Thus far, the story has focused on Boaz as the Christ-figure and husband. But now there is a shift to Obed as the Christ figure, the promised seed of the woman. He will be the one to care for Ruth and Naomi in their old age. He is the replacement for the fallen sons in Ruth 1. The women say, "May his name be famous," recalling God's promise to Abraham to make his name great. This is a true son of Abraham who is going to be made great. His name is not just going to be preserved but exalted.

In Ruth 4:15, they say, "May he be the restorer of Naomi's life and care for her in old age." This is messianic language, echoing language found elsewhere in Scripture. Christ gives us resurrection life and a secure future. That is what Obed is going to do symbolically. We must look at these things typologically, but we must also look at them from a practical angle. It is expected in a biblical culture that children will care for their parents, even grandparents, in their old age; we see this throughout the Scriptures. The elderly were valued. They were not shunned or neglected, but their care is assured through their children

Ruth is also praised in these closing verses. Ruth loves Naomi and is better than seven sons to her. Seven sons, of course, was the Old Testament ideal, but the narrative declares that Ruth is better than seven sons. Sometimes people accuse the Bible of having a patriarchal bias and devaluing women. The Bible teaches us about the differences between men and women, but it does not privilege men in a way that is degrading to women. In fact, the text shows that in this case, one woman is better than seven men. This blessing also indicates a total reversal. Naomi came back with no sons, empty-handed, but she returned with Ruth, with one who would have been better than not just the two sons she lost, or even her husband, a third man, but better than seven men.

Applying the Gospel of Ruth

Some express concern that when we read the Bible through a typological grid, the application of the text may be lost. The question to consider is: "How do you apply this story if it is designed to show us the gospel?" The answer: the gospel is always applicable. How does this story apply? In Ruth 3:18, Naomi says to Ruth, "Wait, my daughter, until you learn how the matter turns out, for the man will not rest but will settle the matter today." The book of Ruth provides similar counsel to the Bride of Christ: "Sit still." Watch the salvation of your God. You can rest because God will see to it, through Jesus Christ, the kinsman-redeemer. The matter of salvation is settled. And God not only gives us his word, as Boaz gave Ruth his word, but he also provides us with a sign, a sacrament, the way Boaz gave Ruth a sign of six handfuls of barley. In Christ, we have something better than six handfuls of barley. We have the sacraments of baptism and the Lord's Supper. These are God's pledges to us that he will see us through and will settle the matter of our redemption.

Other ethical lessons and applications can be drawn from the book of Ruth. The chief one is summed up by the word *hesed*. The best translation is "covenant faithfulness," or "covenant love." It is the manifestation of covenant loyalty. It is a fulfillment of your obligations toward another person. God shows *hesed* to us in the way that he fulfills his covenant. But we, in turn, are to show *hesed* to him and one another. The Book of Ruth embodies this theme; a back and forth volley between the *hesed* of Ruth and the *hesed* of Boaz. Ruth also shows this in the way she covenantally binds herself to Naomi.

Ruth could have thought it was possible to experience a much better future if she stayed in Moab, but somewhere along the way, she picked up enough of the truth to know that Israel's God was the true God. Staying in Moab would be idolatry. So she binds herself in a covenant that is stronger than a marriage covenant. Not just a "till death do us part" covenant, but a bond beyond death. She completely intertwines her future with that of Naomi, which, of course, at the time looks quite bleak. But this is her manifestation of *hesed*. Boaz praises her for her *hesed* in coming back with Naomi. Later when Ruth goes to meet with Boaz on the threshing room floor, he praises her again. He says that this act of *hesed* is even greater than her first act of *hesed*. It was one thing to return with Naomi from Moab to a strange land. But now she outdoes herself, proposing a levirate marriage to Boaz to raise up a replacement for Naomi's deceased husband and deceased sons; that is a great act of *hesed*. Boaz manifests *hesed* as well. He not only allows Ruth to come and glean in his fields, but he gives her special privileges, over and above the standard gleaning opportunities. Later on in the story, Boaz pledges to her that he will see to it she is redeemed. If he cannot do it, he is going to make sure the closer kinsman does it. He is a man of his word and a man of *hesed*.

Helping other covenant members in need is the essence of being faithful to the covenant. Ruth helps Naomi and Boaz helps Ruth and Naomi. This is the flow of the story. Naomi and Ruth were on the brink of poverty and starvation, and Boaz provided for their salvation out of his resources and abundance. We can think of analogies in our personal experience. Sometimes people we know are needy in other ways. They may be lonely or emotionally scarred. They may need someone to come alongside them and encourage them. These are examples of ways we can manifest *hesed* to one another.

❧

THE CHILD'S NAME

The name of the child born to Boaz and Ruth is Obed. The name was not common in Israel. The women of the city gave him the name. The name Obed means "servant." It is probably a shortened form of the name Obadiah, which means "servant of Yahweh." When we think of the servant of the Lord, our thoughts may gravitate to Isaiah and his prophecy of a coming servant who will do the will of the Lord. He will redeem the people by suffering for the people, as Isaiah 53 describes. He will also be victorious, as described in Isaiah 60-62. The name, then, is a messianic title. And this is appropriate because Obed is a type of the Messiah. He is a kind of kinsman-redeemer figure. We can say Jesus is the ultimate Obed.

David himself is referred as the Lord's Obed again and again. In more than thirty times in the Old Testament and several times in the New Testament, the Bible identifies David as the Obed of the Lord. Obeb points ahead to David, who, in turn, leads us to Jesus. Mark 10 says Jesus came not to be served but to be an *Obed* to the people.

❧

Ruth 4:18-22

> Now these are the generations of Perez: Perez fathered Hezron, Hezron fathered Ram, Ram fathered Amminadab, Amminadab fathered Nahshon, Nahshon fathered Salmon, Salmon fathered Boaz, Boaz fathered Obed, Obed fathered Jesse, and Jesse fathered David.

The book ends with a genealogy. This is not merely an appendix tacked on to the end of the narrative. Instead, it is the climax of the story. Some have suggested this genealogy is a later addition, but the most natural reading indicates the genealogy was included from the beginning because it is integral to the meaning of the book. It gives the book its coherent theological meaning. Without this genealogy at the end, the book of Ruth is a beautiful story, but probably not worthy of inclusion in the canon.

The last word in the book is the name "David," after a recounting of ten generations. The book of Ruth connects historically with the end of the book of Judges. Remember, Ruth is set in the era of the Judges, and it is an answer to the problems that have been identified in the book of Judges. Judges ends with God's people in need of a king. The book of Ruth ends with the name David, showing us the prototypical king.

David also is a part of the first generation of Judahite sons — since Perez, the illegitimate son who could not enter the assembly of the Lord —who would have been eligible to enter the assembly and hold office in Israel. As a descendent of Judah, David will hold the scepter (Gen. 49:10).

The ten-generation list in the book of Ruth also alludes to the genealogies in the book of Genesis. In Genesis, there are two passages with ten-generation lists (Genesis 5 and Genesis 11). The genealogy in Genesis 5 ends with Noah and the one in Genesis 11 culminates with Abraham. For David, this genealogy puts him in the same redemptive-historical role as Noah and Abraham. Just as those new men were new Adam figures who began new phases in history, so David will start a new phase of history for the people of God. The Hebrew word *toledoth* used in Ruth 4 to introduce the genealogy is the word that Genesis uses at several points along the way to introduce new stories. It is the word used in Genesis 5 and Genesis 11 where ten-generation lists are given. The book of Ruth functions as a new Genesis. Ruth is the eighth book in the Hebrew canon; the number eight signifying new creation. The people of God are entering into a new creation through David. David is a new Noah figure and a new Abraham figure. He is a king and a prophet, and he will begin Israel's history all over.

Appendix A

TOWARD A THEOLOGY OF THE LAND

———— ❧❧❧ ————

Let's say you were reading your Bible continuously from Judges to Ruth. At the end of the book of Judges you read this refrain: "In those days there was no king in Israel; everyone did what was right in his own eyes." Then you come across this at the beginning of Ruth: "Now it came to pass, in the days when the judges ruled, that there was a famine in the land. And a certain man of Bethlehem went to dwell in the country of Moab, he and his wife and his two sons." At this time in history, during the period of the judges, everyone is doing what is right in his own eyes. That is what happens in the book of Ruth: Elimelech takes his family out of the land of promise and goes down to Moab. Rather than repenting in the land, he goes into self-imposed exile outside the land.

Does it matter that Elimelech left the land of promise? What role did the land have in the Old Testament? In our time, Christians do not treat any particular piece of ground as holy, because God does not meet us on any particular piece of turf, but wherever two or three gather in his name. In fact, the Christian faith is perhaps the only major world religion not tied to a specific place. For the most part, other religions are bound to the area in which they originated. For example, Buddhism has remained primarily Asian and Islam primarily Middle Eastern. Even when a Muslim does leave the Middle East, he is still tied to Mecca in some way. His faith is geographically bounded. Likewise, Jews who live outside the land of Israel often take pilgrimages, because their faith is tied to a specific piece of real estate that is considered holier than other places.

But this is not the case with the Christian faith. The church has no geographic center. It is a faith continually on the move. Yes, the church started out in Jerusalem, but the Christian population quickly moved northward and westward into the Mediterranean area. Later, the church gravitated toward Western Europe and North America. Now the church is exploding in the global South and China. The church is not tied to one place any more than it is tied to one language or one culture.

LAND OF CONFUSION

To fully understand the role of the land in Ruth 1, we need to complete a biblical-theological survey. Let's start with the land of Palestine. This land certainly had a special status during a particular period of history in the Old Covenant, before Christ came. But is it still special or unique in some way today?

There is a lot of confusion about Palestine in today's church. As a result, many of our politicians are muddled in their thinking about Middle Eastern politics. The Israeli geopolitical state has no special covenant status, no special promises, and should be treated by Christians as just another nation. America may or may not find Israel to be a helpful ally, but there is no theological reason why Israel should be favored above any other nation that denies Christ. If America sustains an alliance with Israel, it should be because Israel shares more of our cultural values and economic interests than the other nations in the region, though it should remain a Christian concern that evangelism is forbidden by Israeli law.

Several questions can be raised: Why did the land have special status under the Old Covenant and not under the new? Is there any typological counterpart to the Old Covenant holy land in the New Covenant? Does the loss of a special holy land mean that the transition from Old Covenant to New Covenant entails a shift from the physical to the non-physical? The following seven propositions are set forth to answer these questions. These seven propositions will take us through the history of the land of promise.

First, the land was included in God's promise to Abraham. We see this promise reiterated again and again (Gen. 12:1; Gen. 15:18; Gen. 17:8). The land is one of the blessings that God promises to bestow upon Abraham and his descendants. Of course, in light of the story of Genesis, this has to be seen as a renewal or a restoration of the Garden of Eden. Adam got kicked out of the Garden of Eden, but now God promises to restore possession of the garden sanctuary. He will reverse Adam's exile.

Second, while Abraham and other patriarchs wandered in the land occasionally as resident aliens, the land finally became the full possession of Abraham's descendants after the exodus. Joshua led the conquest of the land, and this became a distinguishing privilege for Israel: to dwell in the place where God had put his name, in the new Eden. Gentiles could come and dwell in the land, but even then the Gentiles could not become permanent residents because portions of the land reverted to the previous owner every so often under the laws God gave to his people. The land was an ongoing possession for Israel, and Gentiles could not live in it in the same way. Of course, the vast majority of Gentiles were excluded altogether. This does not mean Gentiles could not be saved in the Old Covenant. The book of Ruth disproves that point since Ruth herself is a Gentile. Indeed, there are other examples of Gentile God-fearers in the Old Covenant.[10] However, regarding nearness to God and special covenant privileges, these blessings belong to Israel and not to the nations in the Old Covenant era.

---

10   Gentile God-fearers are Gentiles who worshiped the God of Israel

Third, in Deut. 28:64-66, God promised to drive the people of Israel from the land if they were unfaithful:

> And the LORD will scatter you among all peoples, from one end of the earth to the other, and there you shall serve other gods of wood and stone, which neither you nor your fathers have known. And among these nations you shall find no respite, and there shall be no resting place for the sole of your foot, but the LORD will give you there a trembling heart and failing eyes and a languishing soul. Your life shall hang in doubt before you. Night and day you shall be in dread and have no assurance of your life.

Indeed, that is what happened. It first occurred in northern Israel in 722 B.C., and then it happened to Judah in the south in 586 B.C. The point is that the holy land cannot tolerate an unholy people.

Fourth, the same prophets who announced that exile was imminent also promised a return from exile in a new exodus. Just as the first exodus led to their possession of the land, so the prophets described a return to the land by using the language of a new exodus. This happened in some sense under emperor Cyrus around 516 B.C. Ezra, Nehemiah, Haggai, and other Old Testament books describe the people being restored to the land. There is another conquest of sorts. The temple is rebuilt, and the people dwell in the land once again. But not all Israelites returned, and Israel was never a geopolitical entity, at least never for very long. She never had the kind of geopolitical independence she had earlier in her history under the glorious reigns of King David and King Solomon. In the Restoration Covenant (as this era is best called), Israel's glory was greater but also more hidden than before, and, while Israel's home base was certainly Jerusalem, the nation continued to interact heavily with the Gentile nations in a missional way. God was housing his people in a Gentile empire.

---

without becoming Jews.

Fifth, in A.D. 70 the Israelites were again driven from the land and scattered through the nations. This judgment was punishment for crucifying Jesus and persecuting his church. What happened in A.D. 70 was significant because it ended Israel's special status as God's chosen nation. The royal priesthood was taken from Israel and given to a new people who would bear its fruits, which is the new Israel (Gal. 6:16). The events of AD 70 marked the end of the old creation, with a centrally located sanctuary.

Jesus makes many predictions in the gospel accounts about the destruction of the temple and its consequences. These predictions are clear in the Olivet Discourse found in Matthew 24, Mark 13, and Luke 21. His disciples are greatly impressed as they are walking around the buildings in Jerusalem. They to say Jesus, "Look at these marvelous buildings." To this Jesus replies, "Not one stone is going to be left on another." He then launches into a description of how the temple will be dismantled by the Romans as a judgment of God. This is not just any ordinary judgment; this is judgment on the entirety of the Old Covenant order. In Matthew 23, Jesus says the current generation of Jews would be held accountable for all the righteous blood that had been shed, not only under the Mosaic covenant but actually going all the way back to Abel, the first martyr in history (Matt. 23:35-36). The entire old creation era, stretching from the creation of the world up through AD 70, comes to an end when the temple is destroyed. The whole system of the old creation, which included circumcision, the Jew/Gentile division, the sacrificial system, a lunar-regulated calendar, and the sacred geographic space (and all the laws pertaining to that space) in Palestine, would come to an end. Thus, we must conclude that the land of Palestine has no more special standing, certainly no more than circumcision in the New Covenant era. The land no longer possesses covenantal significance. There is nothing special about that particular piece of real estate in the Middle East. That whole system has been fulfilled and judged and done away with.

Finally, we must say that God's covenant with his people continues to be tied to their inheritance of land. It is not as though we have moved beyond the land to an ethereal, immaterial hope. Rather, in the New Covenant, the land promise has been *expanded* to include the whole earth. Now the whole world is declared holy in Christ. The land in Palestine that God promised to Abraham was just a down payment on a much greater inheritance, namely, the whole cosmos. Israel's conquest and possession of the land was a foreshadowing of a much greater inheritance God would give to his people. The church is destined to inherit the earth as she grows and disciples the nations of the earth. When Christ returns, he will completely free this physical creation from the effects of sin and the fall, and we will dwell with God in a renovated physical creation for all eternity. That and nothing less is the biblical hope held out before us. Just as we will be resurrected and live for all eternity in resurrection bodies, so the creation itself will undergo a kind of resurrection. Revelation 21-22 describe heaven and earth being merged together. This is the vision we should have: heaven and earth will become one. That was always God's intention: to marry himself to his people and to make heaven and earth one. This is the final blessed hope of God's people.

Our hope is not only eternal, but it is also historical. Even now the church is promised that "the meek will inherit the earth." Even now the promise God made to Abraham of a global family is coming to pass. This promise is consistent with the Great Commission to go and disciple the nations (Matt. 28:18-20). In the Great Commission, Jesus says, in essence, "I promised you the whole world; now go and claim it. Go get what is yours." The church's commission is to go and fill the earth with Christ's disciples. But the command is backed by a promise. The promise God has given to us includes not just a piece of the earth, but the earth in its entirety. An example of this is Paul's reframing of the fifth commandment in Ephesians 6. Whereas Jewish children under the Old Covenant were promised long life in the land of promise, Christian children in Ephesus are promised a long life in the *earth*. The promise applies not just to Jewish children in the land of promise but to Gentile children wherever they live. The scope of the promise has moved from a narrow piece of land to cover the whole world, just as it has expanded from Jewish children to Gentile Christian children.

INTERPRETING THE LAND THROUGH DISPENSATIONAL LENSES

There are two common mistakes made concerning the land. The first mistake comes from looking at the land of promise through the lens of dispensational theology. Dispensationalism is certainly not as popular as it once was, but it is still pervasive in some segments of the evangelical church, and certainly continues to exert political influence in America. The mistake of Dispensationalism is to think of the land of Canaan itself (or Palestine, as we call it today) as still special in some way. However, this is an implicit denial of the newness of the New Covenant. It is a denial of the worldwide scope of Christ's work, which brings Jew and Gentile believers together into a common salvation and common inheritance. If Jewish believers in Christ are promised something that Gentile believers are not, then Paul is wrong to claim there is no longer any distinction between Jew and Gentile in Christ.

Paul's epistles show us again and again that there is no difference between Jew and Gentile believers in the New Covenant; we share in the same salvation, the same blessings, and the same ultimate inheritance. This aspect of the New Covenant receives significant focus in the Epistles to the Romans, Galatians, and Ephesians. In Christ, the Jew/Gentile distinction has been abolished; in Christ, we are one. Thus, to say that Jewish believers are owed a special promise of land is a violation of the gospel. It does not make any sense to say Gentile believers in Christ have blessings A and B, but Jewish believers in Christ have blessings A, B, and C. Thus the logic of Dispensationalism, which posits different salvific blessings for Jews and Gentiles, goes completely against the grain of New Testament revelation.

We should no longer refer to the land of Palestine as "holy land" any more than we should refer to circumcision as the sign of God's covenant with his people. Sure, it may be wonderful to go to Palestine for historical reasons. The most important events in the history of humanity happened there. But you are not any nearer to God there than anywhere else. It is not some kind of religious pilgrimage. Jesus said he would be present wherever two or three gathered in his name. In the New Covenant, we do not have to go to the temple; the temple comes to us. The heavenly sanctuary opens to us whenever we call out to the Father in Jesus' name (Heb. 10:19ff).

SPIRITUALIZING AWAY THE LAND AND REDEMPTION

The second mistake is to assume the Old Covenant promise of land has been transformed into the promise of an ethereal heaven in the New Covenant. It is simply wrong-headed to think God's promise no longer takes form in the physical dimension. Sometimes Christians have become more heaven-oriented than land-oriented. We cannot spiritualize away the promises of Scripture. Our final hope as God's people, the covenant people, is not to go to heaven when we die. We certainly go to heaven when we die, but as already discussed, this is what theologians call the intermediate state, not the final phase of our salvation. Sure, going to heaven at death is glorious. Paul says it is better to be with Christ than to be here in the body for now. We will be done with sin and suffering at that point, but Paul also points us to the resurrection of the body (1 Corinthians 15) and the renewal of the cosmos (Rom. 8:17ff) as the church's blessed hope. Heaven is just a holding place until the resurrection at the last day.

What, then, does it mean to be heavenly minded (Col. 3:1-4)? It means we are to focus our hopes on heaven precisely because heaven is where Christ dwells bodily at present. Being heavenly-minded is being Christ-minded. Being heavenly minded, in this sense, does not make us useless on earth. Instead, it empowers us to make earth like heaven — to do God's will on earth as it is in heaven. Ultimately, heaven and earth will be united. The renewed heaven-earth environment is our final destination. Looking up is actually a way of looking ahead. Focusing on heaven is focusing on the future.

Many in the church today need to re-orient their expectations about the future. This is important because what we believe about the future has so many implications for how we live in the here and now. Future expectations shape present actions. Compare someone whose final expectation is to dwell forever in an ethereal heaven with someone whose final hope is the resurrection of the body and a renewed physical creation. Who do you think is more likely to work hard in the body right now? Who do you think is more likely to help the poor, not just preaching to them, but to also meet their physical needs? Who is more likely to match evangelism with social care for people? Obviously, all things being equal, the one who is hoping for the resurrection of the body and the transfiguration of the material world is going to be more motivated to deal holistically with people's needs. If the body will be raised in the future, such an outcome suggests we should have a high view of the body in the present. What you do in the body counts forever.

Paul elaborates on this extensively in 1 Corinthians 15. He defends the resurrection in every aspect. Paul's conclusion to this chapter takes an anti-climatic turn. He says that since we are going to be raised bodily, we are to be steadfast, immovable, always abounding in the work of the Lord, knowing that in the Lord our labor is not in vain (1 Cor. 15:58). The Christian has a future hope of a resurrection body. So what should you do right now? *Get to work.* That is the application Paul draws from the future resurrection. It seems strange. We want to ask, "Paul, is that the best application you can come up with after a 57-verse defense of the resurrection?" But actually, it makes perfect sense. The body you are working in now will be the body you will have for all eternity (albeit transformed and perfected). The creation that you are working in right now to transform will indeed be transfigured and glorified at the last day. All your labors for the Lord and in the Lord will pay off eternally. The Lord will establish the works of our hands forever. God's plan is not for us to sit around on clouds plucking harps. We will live in a perfected new creation, where we will worship, work, and play to perfection.

Abraham had resurrection faith. Where did he find the resolve to take Isaac up on the mount and raise the knife? Of course, as he is about to plunge the knife into his beloved son, God stops him. But how did Abraham go as far as he did? Hebrews 11 tells us that Abraham had the hope of the resurrection. Abraham believed that if he killed Isaac, God would raise him back up. He had already seen God bring life out of death. How did he get Isaac in the first place? God had to first "resurrect" Abraham and Sarah's aging bodies in order to produce Isaac. Abraham believed if God could resurrect the womb of his aged wife, certainly God could resurrect the child himself. That resurrection hope drove Abraham to obedience and shaped his life.

Abraham also knew that God promised him a lot more than the strip of land in Palestine. After all, God promised Abraham a worldwide family: "In you all the families of the earth shall be blessed." That many people would not be able to fit inside the land. Just as he reasoned that God would raise Isaac, he reasoned that the promise of land would extend much, much further than that plot of ground in the Middle East. He knew that God was ultimately going to bless the whole earth; the whole earth would have to become a holy land. Romans 4 confirms Abraham had a global faith, just as Hebrews 11 confirms he had a resurrection faith. Paul says that Abraham was heir of the world (Rom. 4:13).

THE TYPOLOGICAL PURPOSE OF THE
LAND: THE LAND AS CHRIST

There is a three-fold typological dimension to the land. First, we must remember that all typology is ultimately Christology; all types and shadows in the Old Covenant find their fulfillment in Christ. We can draw a line from the land of promise straight to fulfillment in Jesus Christ. In the Old Covenant, to be in the land is tremendously important. But in the New Testament, being in Christ has replaced (or fulfilled) being in the land. According to the book of Joshua and Psalm 95, to be in the land is to enter into God's rest. The land exists in a kind of permanent Sabbath. However, in Matthew 11, Jesus declares that he is the rest. Now, the way to enter God's rest is to enter Christ. The land was entered via a water crossing; likewise, we enter Christ through the waters of baptism.

Why is there is an entire chapter in the book of Genesis exclusively devoted to Abraham's negotiations for a little piece of the land to bury Sarah after she dies? It is because to rest in the land was a sign and a symbol of being in Christ. Of course, he wants his wife to rest there. It was a sign of his faith. Likewise, consider Jacob's charge to his children in Gen. 49:29ff to take his bones back and bury them in the land. Why does it matter? These instructions are a sign of his faith and his longing to be in Christ. The very end of the book of Genesis is about his burial in the land because it is a sign of things to come; it is promissory. To be in the land is (symbolically and sacramentally) a sign of being in Christ.

Thus, to be exiled from the land was a sign of apostasy and exclusion from Christ. The language of the book of Leviticus makes this case. When the people were in sin, the law says the land would vomit them out (Lev. 18:25, 28). A holy land cannot abide an unholy people. But what is the New Covenant counterpart to the land vomiting out apostates? In Revelation 3, Jesus says he will vomit out lukewarm (unfaithful) covenant members. This threat applies to church members who have been incorporated into him, but if they are not faithful, Christ will spit them out of his mouth. What the land would do to unfaithful Israel, now Jesus threatens to do with an unfaithful church.

HOLY DIRT

Remember that the first principle of Augustine's biblical interpretation was *totus Christus*, the total Christ, head and body. Types are fulfilled in Christ but do not terminate with Christ;

they have a "follow through" in Christ's people, the church. So we have to ask, how is the land a type of the church as well? We should think of ourselves as the true holy land. We are the holy land come to life. How did God form the first man? Out of the dust of the ground. What was Adam? Adam was dirt into which God breathed life.

We are made from the dust of the earth. The Scripture says that the serpent's curse was to eat dirt. However, Scripture also tells us Satan is a lion seeking whom he may devour. Satan is looking for some dirt to eat.

What kind of dirt are we? The Bible calls us saints, which means we are holy dirt. We are holy land. We are the living embodiment of the holy land. In the New Covenant, you and your fellow Christians are sacred space. You are the land and the city and the temple.

Consider how sacred space worked in the Old Covenant. The holiness system of the Old Covenant was geographically-based, at least symbolically. If you wanted to get near to God, you went to the temple in Jerusalem. In the New Covenant, Jesus says, "Wherever two or three are gathered in my name, there I am." The sacred place is where we gather. Why? Because we are the sacred space. We have seen that to be in Christ fulfills what it meant for Israel to be in the land. We can also say that to be in the church fulfills the meaning of being in the holy land. The Scriptures points us to this truth rather explicitly. In Heb. 11:16, we are given a summary of what these Old Covenant saints were looking for as they peered into the future with the eyes of faith: "They desire a better country, that is, a heavenly one." Their faith looked beyond the land of Palestine to something greater. "Therefore," Hebrews says, "God is not ashamed to be called their God, for He has prepared a city for them." In Hebrews, this heavenly country and city are virtually interchangeable. So we must ask, "What is the heavenly country?" What is the heavenly city they were promised?" In the New Testament, we find it is the church.

The church is the heavenly Jerusalem (Galatians 4, Revelation 21-22). Hebrews 12 says when we come to church, we come to "Mount Zion and to the city of the living God, the heavenly Jerusalem." What heavenly country and city did the patriarchs long to see? The church. All these geographical and political entities in the Old Covenant find their fulfillment in the community of the New Covenant. The land was once God's dwelling place, the place where he had placed his name; now the church is God's dwelling place, the place where God has put his name.

Finally, we can say the land, typologically considered, was a down payment on the much greater possession that God would give to his people, namely, the whole earth. The whole earth has now been cleansed and is a fit dwelling place for God. To speak of the land of Palestine as "the holy land" is to suggest that the rest of the earth is still unholy and unclean, and therefore under God's curse. If we are tempted to think that way, we need to remember what God said to Cornelius: "Do not call unclean what God has cleansed." Jesus Christ has claimed the entire world. If it does not look holy yet, just wait. It's only a matter of time. The world may not look like a heavenly country or a holy city yet, but God promises to make it so.

The Universality of the Land

In the period during which the story of Ruth takes place, God's presence and promise were in some sense tied to the land of Palestine. Consider the story of Naaman the Syrian, found in 2 Kings 5. Naaman was a Syrian who contracted leprosy. By following the instructions of the prophet Elisha, he is cleansed in the Jordan River. Then he insists on taking some dirt from the promised land back home with him (2 Kings 5:17). That sounds somewhat superstitious to us, and it would be superstitious to do something like that today. But in Naaman's day, it made perfect sense, which is why Elisha blesses his action. At that time, Naaman knew that God's presence and promises were tied to that piece of land. By taking dirt from Israel back home, he is taking

God's holiness and presence with him. It's an act of faith, a sign that he trusts the God of Israel. Of course, it is also typological, foreshadowing the extension of sacred space to the ends of the earth.

Bring all this back to Ruth 1 and Elimelech's decision to leave the land. In the New Covenant, we are free to move about from place to place, nation to nation, without any effect on our relationship with God. We can meet with God anywhere. Of course, there is a sense in which that was true under the Old Covenant. However, it is also true that under the Old Covenant God's land symbolized God's presence, and Israel living in the land was a sign of enjoying God's blessing in a special way. To deliberately leave the land after the conquest was to take the curse of exile upon oneself. Typologically speaking, for Elimelech to exit the land was essentially equivalent to forsaking Christ and the church. Elimelech abandoned his inheritance in the land, which was a sign of abandoning his eternal inheritance. Not surprisingly, living outside the land brought death.

Appendix B

Toward a Theology of Wings

———— ✦ ————

Ruth 2:12 sets the stage for us as Boaz says to Ruth, "The LORD repay your work, and a full reward be given you by the LORD God of Israel, under whose wings you have come for refuge." What does the text mean when it speaks of Ruth coming to find refuge under the wings of the Lord? Boaz prays that Ruth may be rewarded by the Lord under his wings where she has found refuge. What does that tell us about God? What does that say about the nature of our salvation?

Later on in the book (Ruth 3:9), Ruth is going to give Boaz the opportunity to answer his own prayer. On the threshing floor at night, she will come to him and say, "Spread your wing over your maidservant, for you are *go'el*, you are a kinsman-redeemer." What does this wing imagery mean?

To spread the wing over another was to form a covenant bond with another. Ezekiel 16 provides a glimpse into this theme by describing God's marriage to Israel, the way he has bonded himself in love to his people. The passage says that when Israel was born God baptized her; he washed her. This is likely a reference to the exodus and the Red Sea crossing. God washed her in water and then nurtured her so that she grew and matured and became beautiful. Then, when the time was right, he married her. This may be a reference to what happened at Sinai or to some other point in Israel's history when God entered into covenant with her. He swore a marriage oath to her. And in Ezek. 16:8 we are told:

> "When I passed by you again and looked on you, indeed your time was the time of love, so I spread my wing over you and covered your nakedness. Yes, I swore an oath to you and entered into a covenant with you, and you became mine," says the Lord God.

This is a poetic description of God's marriage to Israel. It's as though God is a bird who spreads his wings over his bride to protect and shield her. For God to spread his wing over Israel is to enter into covenant with her. Of course, that is exactly what Ruth asks Boaz to do in Ruth 3. "Spread your wing over me" is basically her way of saying, "Marry me. Make me your own. Take an oath to make me your wife by covenant."

A quick biblical tour of the concept of wings reveals that translators have done us a big disservice by not translating the word consistently. The word translated "wing" in Ruth 2 and Ruth 3 and Ezekiel 16 is sometimes translated in other terms.

The origin of wing imagery begins in the creation account in Genesis 1, where we are told that the Spirit *hovered* or *fluttered* above the watery, unformed, unfilled earth. Already we find bird imagery used to describe God, particularly the Holy Spirit. In Deuteronomy 32, God brings the Israelites out of Egypt, and the text refers to God hovering above the people. It is the same wording used in the creation account of Genesis 1. The exodus is a new creation; Israel becomes like a new creation. Once again, God flutters above his creation, his newly formed people.

Another example of this theme is found in Num. 15:37-41:

> The LORD said to Moses, "Speak to the people of Israel, and tell them to make tassels on the corners of their garments throughout their generations, and to put a cord of blue on the tassel of each corner. And it shall be a tassel for you to look at and remember all the commandments of the LORD, to do them, not to follow after your own heart and your own eyes, which you are inclined to whore after. So you shall remember and do all my commandments, and be holy to your God. I am the LORD your God, who brought you out of the land of Egypt to be your God: I am the LORD your God."

When the text speaks of the *corner* of the garment, it is actually speaking of the *wing* of the garment. Every Israelite was to wear a garment with four corners, or four wings, and on each corner, or wing, of the garment there was to be a tassel of blue. These blue tassels were signs or memorials to the Lord and to the covenant that he had made with Israel. Perhaps you have heard of "blue laws," like Sabbath laws, for example. It seems these blue laws originated with the Scottish Covenanters, who chose to use the color blue as their symbol of the covenant. Presbyterians in Scotland became known as people who were *true blue* (an expression still used).

The Israelites had blue tassels on each corner, or wing, of their garments to remind them of their covenant with God and how they were to be loyal to him. Their wings served as constant symbolic reminders that they were his special people, that they had been redeemed in the exodus. They were his heavenly people (blue is the color of the heavens, of course).

In Ezek. 1:6, we find the cherubim, the angelic guardians of God's throne, have four wings. If an Israelite wears a garment with four wings, we can immediately see a connection between the individual Israelite and a cherub. The primary function of the cherubim was to guard the holiness of God (e.g., there were gold cherubim on the Ark of the Covenant guarding the Shekinah glory of God). Israel, in a sense, was to be a nation of cherubim. They were to be a cherubim-like people, a royal priesthood guarding the throne and holiness of God.

In Ezek. 1:8, there is a symbolic connection made between the wings of the cherubim and their hands. Of course, hands throughout Scripture have to do with power, authority, and help. In Haggai 2, there is also a parallel made between the wings — actually in that particular context, the wings of the garment — and the hands of the person. It is as though the wings on the garments are symbolic hands. They are symbolic of power, authority, and help.

There are also numerous passages throughout the Psalter and the Prophets that speak of God having wings. Some of these passages are among the most beautiful and poetic texts in all of Scripture. Psalm 17:8, for example, says, "Keep me as the apple of your eye; hide me under the shadow of your wings." Just as one would do anything to protect the apple of one's eye, so those who dwell under the shadow of God's wings are in a place of protection.

Psalm 36:7 says, "How precious is your loving-kindness, O God. Therefore the children of men put their trust under the shadow of your wings." So, God's loving-kindness, his *hesed*, is strong, unbreakable covenant love. What does it mean to be shielded and sheltered by that covenant love? It means total safety and security. To have been brought under the protection of God's wings is glorious. It is salvation. As Psalm 57:1 says, "Be merciful to me, O God, be merciful to me. For my soul trusts in you; and in the shadow of your wings I will make my refuge, until these calamities have passed me by." Where do you hide in time of calamity and time of distress and trouble? You take refuge under the wings of God. There you find his mercy and provision.

In Psalm 61:4, David says, "I will abide in your tabernacle forever; I will trust in the shelter of your wings." Of course, David was a king, not a priest, so he couldn't abide in the tabernacle at all. David is speaking eschatologically by looking ahead to the New Covenant when we have all been brought into the temple presence of God. This is equivalent to taking shelter under the wings of God. To be under the wings of God is to be incorporated into his tabernacle or his temple presence. There is a kind of nearness to God that comes with this.

Another example is found in Psalm 63:7: "For you have been my help, and in the shadow of your wings I will sing for joy." So the wing is a place of help; it is the place where God's power is manifest for our protection. In a similar manner, see Psalm 91:4: "He will cover you with his pinions, and under his wings you will find refuge; his faithfulness is a shield and buckler." God is like a mighty bird who swoops down over us and protects us and shields us with his wings.

Moving into the New Testament, Jesus picks up on this theme as a part of his teaching as well. For example, in Matt. 23:37, in the context of all the curses he pours out upon the Pharisees, he looks toward Jerusalem and says, "O Jerusalem, Jerusalem, the one who kills the prophets and stones those who are sent to her. How often I wanted to gather your children together, as a hen gathers her chicks under her wings, but you were not willing." Then it says, "See. Your house" — that is, the temple — "is left desolate; for I say to you, you shall see me no more till you say, 'Blessed is he who comes in the name of the Lord.'" Our Lord weeps over Jerusalem because it is a wicked, rebellious city. It has killed the prophets in the past and is about to crucify Jesus who is the ultimate and final prophet. Jesus says, "I long to cover you over with my wings as a hen does her chicks. That's been my desire, to shield you and protect you." Like God in the Old Testament, Jesus has wings.

There are other passages that do not use this particular vocabulary but are clearly related. For example, Psalm 133 speaks of the priest being anointed and the anointing oil flowing down over the priest, down Aaron's beard, all the way down to the edge of his garment, to the very hem of his robe. But, of course, that means to the wings of the garment. The garment itself is symbolic of the people. It means the people, as a whole, are going to be covered with this priestly anointing.

Other passages factor into this as well. In 1 Samuel 15, when Saul is rejected as king over Israel, he seizes the wing, or the corner, of Samuel's robe, and tears it. And Samuel says, "Just as you have torn my robe, so the kingdom has been torn from you." That is to say, tearing the corner of the robe meant that the kingdom was torn from Saul. He lost his authority as the ruler of the kingdom. Later on, in 1 Samuel 24, David secretly comes to Saul in a cave, he sneaks to a place near Saul, and he cuts off the wing of his robe, which is a highly symbolic act.

The wing symbolizes the kingdom; it symbolizes Saul's cherubim-type status as ruler over the kingdom. David taking the corner of the garment is a symbol that David will take the kingdom from Saul. David later repents of this act because he knows he has attacked the authority of the Lord's anointed prematurely. David has to wait on God's timing to receive the kingdom. He recognizes seizing the wing was a dishonorable act. But the point remains that the kingdom's going to be taken from Saul and given to David.

So what have we seen so far? The corner (wing) of the garment represents the covenant. It represents righteousness and protection. It is associated with a person's hand, which has to do with power, authority, and help, and with the kingdom. All these things merge together in this wing theme.

In Ruth 3, Ruth is going to lay hold of the wing of a Jewish man. She is going to receive blessing and protection in this way. In Ruth 2, she takes shelter under the wing of the Lord, and in Ruth 3, she takes hold of Boaz's rule and finds covenant security there.

We are building a composite picture of all that is associated with this wing imagery, and there are certainly other things we could add to this list. But there's one story in particular in the New Testament that brings all of this together. In Luke 8:40-55, we read of a woman who had a flow of blood for twelve years. Of course, this flow of blood made her ritually unclean under Old Testament law. Under the Levitical code, when blood flows out, life is flowing out, and the result is (symbolic) death. The woman in Luke 8 is a walking dead woman. She is unclean or symbolically dead, which means she is excluded from worship ✓ in Israel. Her life has been a living hell. For twelve years, she had been in exile; she had been cut off from the covenant community, unable to attend temple worship. What is worse, she could not have any real fellowship with people because, as an unclean person, everything she touched became unclean. Her uncleanness would spread to others. In the Old Covenant, death spreads (Rom. 5:12ff). Because she has had the flow of blood for twelve years, we might be justified in seeing her condition as a picture of the twelve tribes of Israel under the law, lifeless and unclean.

What does she do? As Jesus walks by, she comes up from behind and touches the winged tassel of Jesus' garments. She grabbed hold of him by his wing. We should think of Zechariah 8, and perhaps also Mal. 4:2. This is probably the passage she held in the back of her mind. She knows she will find healing in the wings of the "Sun of righteousness." Of course, according to Old Testament law what should have happened when this unclean woman touched Jesus is that her uncleanness should have spread to him. He should have become defiled at that point. But instead of her uncleanness and death spreading to him, his holiness spreads to her and overcomes her death.

So, with the coming of Jesus, the whole system in which death spreads to all men is reversed. Now holiness and life and righteousness spread because Jesus has come and the Spirit has come. In Luke 8:46, Jesus says, "power went out from me." And he wants to know who has touched him. In Luke, power is almost always associated with the Holy Spirit. It is as though when this woman touches him, the Holy Spirit flows out through the edge of his garment into this woman and restores her, bringing life to her and overcoming the death that had been flowing out from her. This woman finds healing in the wings of Jesus

Appendix C

GRACE AND GOOD WORKS: A THEOLOGICAL OVERVIEW

In Ruth 2, Ruth makes it very clear she is astonished by Boaz's grace. She asks, "Why have I found favor in your eyes?" Boaz responds in Ruth 2:11 with language that indicates Ruth is like Abraham: she has left her homeland and come to a people/land she did not know. In Ruth 2:12, Boaz says, "The LORD repay you for what you have done, and a full reward be given you by the LORD, the God of Israel, under whose wings you have come to take refuge."

Boaz describes the reward Ruth will receive as a payment. "The LORD repay your work." How should we understand that? What does it mean for the Lord to *repay* our work? Does it mean that when we do good works for God, we're paying God — like putting a coin in the slot — so that God must then pay us back as the reward pops out? Do our works pay God? Do we do work for God so that God gives us a paycheck in return? Is that the kind of relationship described here?

To be sure, Boaz also says Ruth has taken refuge under the wings of the Lord. We saw already that this is the language of a deep covenant relationship, akin to that of a husband and wife.

It is the language of love and faith and grace. But we still have to ask this question: Why this language of repayment in Ruth 2:12? How does it fit?

This is not the only place where this kind of language occurs. Under the New Covenant, Heb. 6:9-10 says:

> Though we speak in this way, yet in your case, beloved, we feel sure of better things—things that belong to salvation. [10] For God is not unjust so as to overlook your work and the love that you have shown for his name in serving the saints, as you still do. [11] And we desire each one of you to show the same earnestness to have the full assurance of hope until the end, [12] so that you may not be sluggish, but imitators of those who through faith and patience inherit the promises.

Paul (or some other inspired writer) says God is not *unjust* to forget the saints' labor of love. What could this possibly mean and how does it square with what we know of God's grace and justice?

Hebrews 6 says God is not going to be unjust; his justice includes regarding those who have labored in love. God is not going to forget to pay them back, we could say, for the work they have done for him. The reward given for works performed is considered a matter of justice (much as it is considered a matter of payment in Ruth 2).

There are some in church history who have taken this as a kind of debt and repayment system. Our sins are debts, our good works are payment, and hopefully things will balance out in our favor in the end, with more credits than debits. But we know that everything in the Bible speaks against such an interpretation. But we still have to ask, "How do we explain this language?" Unless we want to conclude that Boaz is a heretic — perish the thought — we need to understand how his declaration fits into an orthodox soteriological framework.

The key to the language of repayment is that when you walk with God, you walk in the way of obedience. And as you walk in the way of obedience, you find God's blessing, favor, and reward. The blessing is not in any way earned. There is no merit theology in the Bible. There is nothing we can earn from God, no way to purchase God's favor by our good works. We cannot pry God's favor out of heaven. The language of repayment must be understood as covenantal language. It is God's way of saying that those who faithfully walk in obedience are walking in the way of salvation, and God will make good on his promises to them.

Nothing here is incompatible with grace. But biblical grace, true grace, not only grants free forgiveness but also brings transformation. By grace, we are saved apart from works. And by grace, we begin to do good works. By grace, we are forgiven. And by grace, we are changed. By grace, we are accepted. And by grace, our good-but-imperfect works are accepted and rewarded as well. The Westminster Larger Catechism (32) calls this "holy obedience" in which his people walk "the way which he hath appointed them to salvation."

John Calvin observes, "God examines our works according to his tenderness, not his supreme right."[11] If God were to examine our works by a standard of absolute righteousness, our works would always come up short, and they would always be condemned. No matter how much good you are doing right at a given moment, you are not doing it perfectly to the glory of God, and perfectly out of a mature faith, and perfectly out of love. So it would be worthy only of condemnation if judged by God's supreme right. But how does God judge his own people, who are united to his Son by faith? He is a father to his people. Calvin says that God judges them as a father judges the work of a child. He judges the works of his people with a certain tenderness. "Therefore," Calvin says, "he accepts their works as though they were perfectly pure. And for this reason, although unmerited,

---

11   John Calvin, *Institutes of the Christian Religion*, trans. by Ford Lewis Battles (Philadelphia: Westminster Press, 1960), 3.15.4.

they're rewarded with infinite benefits both of the present life and also of the life to come."[12] Calvin understands salvation, in a certain sense, as a reward for good works.

Some will say that this language about repayment has to do with God giving temporal benefits in this life as a reward for good works. Sometimes they point to the book of Proverbs and assert that if you are godly you will experience God's blessings in this life. But such passages, they argue, have nothing to do with salvation. This view actually strays dangerously close to the "prosperity gospel." Plenty of people obey God but do not experience earthly blessing.

Besides, this is not what Calvin says. He says these good works can certainly be rewarded with benefits in the present life at times, but are especially rewarded in the life to come. Calvin notes:

> For I do not accept the distinction made by learned and otherwise godly men that good works deserve the graces that are conferred upon us in this life while everlasting salvation is the reward of faith alone.[13]

Calvin says everlasting salvation is not the reward of faith alone; it is the reward of a working, loving faith, or faith and its fruit. At the same time, Calvin guards himself from a certain misunderstanding. According to Calvin, it would be contrary to Scripture to claim that works merit anything:

> Whatever, therefore, is given to these works is of God's pure grace. Yet, both in this blessedness and in those Godly persons, he takes works into account. For in order to testify to the greatness of his love toward us, he makes not only us but the gift he has given us, worthy of such honor.

---

12 Ibid.

13 Ibid.

The word "worthy" plays a central role in Calvin's language. It is also a crucial category in Scripture. In Revelation 4, the living creatures cry out that the Lamb (Jesus Christ) is worthy to receive glory, honor and power. In Revelations 5, the Lamb is again declared worthy to receive power, riches, and wisdom. Jesus has this worth — indeed, infinite worth. But what's striking is that the works of the saints are described as "worthy" in Rev. 3:4: "Yet you have still a few names in Sardis, people who have not soiled their garments, and they will walk with me in white, for they are worthy." The same word that the saints and the angels use to describe God's worth is the word that God uses to describe the good works of his people. That does not mean one can equate God's worthiness and the works of the saints. If we talk about God's love for us and our love for God, we don't mean the same thing by "love" in those two contexts. But there is a connection. That is precisely what is going on here. Jesus, in his person and work, has infinite worth. Because of our covenant union with Jesus, our good works have worth as well.

Calvin says, "The promise of the gospel not only makes us acceptable to God, but also renders our works pleasing to him."[14] This is good news. God is pleased with our good works. The promise of the gospel is that God will not only accept our persons in Christ, he will also accept our good works for the sake of Christ. Again, Calvin writes:

> Not only does the Lord adjudge them pleasing, he also extends to them the blessings which, under the covenant, were owed to the observance of the law. I therefore admit that the Lord has promised in his law to the keepers of righteousness and holiness a reward is paid to believers. But in this repayment we must always consider the reason that wins favor for these. Now we see that there are three reasons. The first is, God having turned his gaze from his works, which always deserve reproof rather than praise, he embraces his servants in Christ, and reconciles them to himself without the

---

14   Ibid., 3.17.3.

help of works. The second is, of God's own fatherly generosity and loving-kindness and without considering their merit, he raises works to this place of honor so that he attributes some value to them. He receives these very works with pardon, not imputing the imperfection with which they are all corrupted, that they would otherwise be reckoned as sins rather than virtues. To sum up, by this passage he means nothing else but that God's children are pleasing and lovable to him, since he sees in them the marks and features of his own countenance. For we elsewhere have taught that regeneration is a renewal of the divine image in us. Since, therefore, God contemplates his own face, he both rightly loves it and holds it in honor. It is said with good reason that the lives of believers framed to holiness and righteousness are pleasing to him.[15]

It is often said that even our best works are sinful in God's sight, and of course, that is true. In the Protestant tradition, we emphasize that the law of God demands absolute holiness and absolute righteousness, so anything less is only going to be condemned before the bar of God's judgment. That is true for those who are outside of Christ. But that is certainly not the primary way that God would have us think of his law as believers. We should think of the law of God not as a condemning standard so much — although it will condemn us if we are outside of Christ and don't have his forgiveness — but as first and foremost as fatherly instruction.

Many Christians believe they can never do anything good enough for God. Just as children who grow up believing they can never please their earthly fathers end up with deep insecurity, so there are many Christians who view their heavenly Father as impossible to please. But this is not how God wants us to view him. God is pleased and smiles upon us when we are seeking to be obedient, even though he knows our obedience is not perfect. Through the mediation of Christ, the imperfections of our good works are forgiven (just as our sins are forgiven) and the good works we do are accepted by the Father on account of the Son.

---

15   Ibid.

There is a two-fold dynamic taking place in Ruth 2 (and other similar portions of Scripture). What do the saints say when they are ushered into God's presence? We will say, "We are unprofitable servants" (Luke 17:10). We don't have anything to offer to God that could indebt him to us. But what does God say about us? He will say, "Well done, my good and faithful servant" (Matt. 25:23). What should you say about your works? "I am an unprofitable servant, with no merit to offer." That's what Ruth says about her works: "I'm not worthy." But what does God say about your work? He says the same thing that Boaz says: "The Lord is going to repay you. Well done, good and faithful servant." This is the dynamic of the Bible.

⎯⎯•⎯ ⚬⊱•⊰⚬ ⎯•⎯⎯

LAW AND GOSPEL PARADIGM--A THEOLOGICAL OVERVIEW

The language of repayment in Ruth 2 is thus a gospel promise. God will pay her back for her service. We know that because in the immediately preceding verse in 2:11, we read that Boaz answered Ruth saying: "All that you have done for your mother-in-law since the death of your husband has been fully told to me, and how you left your father and mother and your native land and came to a people that you did not know before." Boaz says the Moabitess is just like father Abraham who left his homeland and, in faith, came to a strange land that he did not know. Ruth has demonstrated covenant faithfulness in caring for her mother-in-law. She has essentially become a member of the covenant nation by linking herself to Naomi. It is in the context of this relationship that Boaz says to her, "You're going to be paid back."

But this still sounds strange to our ears, to speak of the Lord paying us back. We would be much more likely to say, "May the Lord be gracious to you" or "May the Lord show you mercy." We would not be so inclined to say, "May the Lord pay you back" or "May the Lord show you justice." If anything, those might be things that we're inclined to say to our enemies. God's going to pay you back for the bad things that you've done. Or, God's going to show you justice for the wicked things that you've done. But in Ruth 2, the language of paying back and of justice is not a threat but an encouragement.

Boaz's reference to repayment is one of those places where certain paradigms or frameworks prove an obstacle to actually understanding the texts of Scripture. And one of those troublesome paradigms is the so-called law/gospel paradigm. The law/gospel paradigm certainly predates the Reformation, but Martin Luther greatly popularized it. Luther was not always consistent in how he worked it out, but in many cases, Luther saw the law as a bad thing and the gospel as a good thing. All the law does is condemn; all the gospel does is give free and unconditional promises. The law is full of threats, and the gospel is this pure, unconditional message of good news, according to Luther. We can certainly say that if someone's trying to earn their own salvation, then the law is going to do nothing but condemn that person. But the gospel condemns that person as well. The gospel becomes an aroma of death to the unbeliever.

Of course, the gospel also makes demands. The gospel requires a response of obedient faith. Yes, this response is itself a gift of God's grace, but it is a response we must make nonetheless.

TOWARD A PROPER UNDERSTANDING OF WORKS

When we see passages like the one in Ruth 2 — "the Lord pay you back" — it does not mean that God is offering salvation as some bargain. In the late medieval church, some believed that if we do enough good works, God will pay us back with salvation. But that law was somewhat relaxed. The law didn't demand perfection; God relaxed his demands to fit with our (natural) abilities. Thus, salvation could be had at a discount rate. But this is a deeply flawed model of salvation. The medieval view had taken a Biblical truth and distorted it.

A more accurate way of understanding the biblical language would be to say that on the basis of Christ's death, resurrection and intercession, our works can be regarded as good and holy in

God's sight, and therefore God can justly pay us back for those works with salvation and with eternal compensation. God does not relax his law as such; rather, he views our works in light of our union with Christ.

Calvin's doctrine of two-fold justification, or a two-fold acceptance, is helpful here. First, our persons are justified apart from works, by faith alone in Christ alone. But following this, there is a second justification of our works, or according to our works. In view of our union with Christ, the Father accepts the works of believers as if they were perfect. Calvin writes:

> But we, on the other hand, without reference to merit still remarkably cheer and comfort the hearts of believers by our teaching when we tell them that they please God in their works and are without doubt acceptable to him.[16]

This truth is something that we need to know, for cheer, for joy, for comfort, for assurance. We must know our works are pleasing to God.

In the book of Ruth, Boaz tells Ruth her works have found God's favor. She ought to rejoice in knowing that God is smiling over her, and that God is pleased with the *hesed* she has shown to Naomi. Now, is Ruth perfect? We wouldn't say she is sinlessly perfect. We know there must have been days when she got frustrated with Naomi, days when she didn't live out *hesed* as perfectly as she might have. But the overall course or pattern of her life is pleasing to God and meets with his favor.

This is the way we should view our lives as well. If we are walking in faith, our walk is pleasing to God. We are walking in the right direction. This does not necessarily mean that every individual step that we've ever taken is pleasing to God, but our overall life's course and direction delight him. If you were to take a host of individual pictures, you might find snapshots of your life that are displeasing to God. But a video of your life would

---

16   Calvin, *Institutes*, 3.15.4.

reveal you are headed in the right direction, even if it happens in fits and starts. This is what it means to be a Christian: you are growing, however slowly, toward godliness.

In the movie *Chariots of Fire*, Eric Liddell says he feels God's pleasure as he runs. We ought to feel God's pleasure whenever we are running in the right direction. Whenever we are not engaged in some overt sinful activity, we should know God is smiling over us. Sure, even our best works always leave something to be desired; they never perfectly conform to God's standards. They could always be reproved or corrected in some way. But God is still pleased with them. God's evaluation of our works is not all or nothing; it's not pass/fail, where any score less than 100% is damned. No, as Calvin says, God judges us according to his own fatherly generosity and loving-kindness.

The Westminster Confession of Faith's Chapter 16 presents a helpful section on good works. It makes the same point that Calvin makes: our good works are acceptable to God because Christ is continually interceding on our behalf. We offer our imperfect good works to God, but before they gets to God, they go through Jesus and he fills up what is lacking and covers over what is impure.

It's interesting to consider how James describes judgment. Jas. 2:13 says, "For judgment is without mercy to the one who has shown no mercy. Mercy triumphs over judgment." Judgment is without mercy to those who show no mercy. But then the flip side must be true: those who do show mercy will be judged mercifully in turn. Had Ruth shown mercy? Yes, she had shown mercy. Because she showed mercy to Naomi, she, in turn, is judged mercifully. Jesus taught the same truth in the Lord's Prayer: "Forgive us our debts as we forgive our debtors." As you are a forgiving person, you can be sure that God will be forgiving toward you. There's a kind of *lex talonis*, eye for eye, tooth for tooth analogy here, but in reverse: It's mercy for mercy. If you show mercy, God is going to show mercy to you. God will deal with you in the same kind of way you deal with others.

What else can we say about this? This is a rather large, biblical theme that shows up in a lot of places, but never gets the attention it deserves. Consider a couple of other passages. In Genesis 22, God is dealing with Abraham. The Abrahamic covenant is considered the paradigm for the covenant of grace throughout Scripture, and yet listen to what God says in Gen. 22:15-18:

> Then the Angel of the Lord called to Abraham a second time out of heaven, and said, "By Myself I have sworn, says the Lord, because you have done this thing, you have not withheld your son, your only son – blessing I will bless you, and multiplying I will multiply your descendants as the stars of the heaven and as the sand which is on the   seashore; and your descendants shall possess the gate of their enemies. In your seed all the nations of the earth shall be blessed, because you have obeyed My voice."

This is the covenant of grace, yet God is saying *because* Abraham has obeyed, he will be blessed. His obedience does not merit blessing, but obedience is the way to enter the blessing.

Psalm 18 is a Psalm of David. In verse 20, we read, "The Lord rewarded me according to my righteousness; according to the cleanness of my hands He has recompensed me." David says the Lord has paid him back for his righteousness. This is the same kind of language found in Ruth 2. If you weren't familiar with this psalm and a fellow Christian told you, "The Lord has recompensed me according to my righteousness," what would you would say? You'd probably exclaim, "You've got it all wrong. That's not how this works. Everything we get from God is a free gift. God's never paying us back according to our righteousness." And yet, here it is in the Bible.

Ultimately, the words of the psalmist are the words of Christ. In the end, the Psalms must be read as the prayers and songs of Christ himself. But we also have to do justice to the original, historical meaning of the psalm as well. David wrote the words in Psalm 18 and meant them. But what did he mean by them? Is he claiming sinless perfection? No, we can rule that out fairly quickly. We know elsewhere that David confesses he is a sinner and was a sinner from birth. What is he actually claiming when he says he has been righteous? He is claiming covenant faithfulness. He is not saying that he's lived perfectly in every respect, but the basic direction of his life is one of covenant loyalty, which means he seeks to obey God. Of course, this also means when he fails, he confesses his sin, seeks God's forgiveness, and moves forward in repentance.

Again, we have to ask, in what sense can the imperfect good works that we do be worthy of blessing, reward and repayment? In what sense can all of this be a matter of justice? Again, too often we have thought of God's justice only as something to fear. Because God is just, he must punish our sin. We've almost made God's justice synonymous with his wrath. But if we look at the way justice language is used in Scripture, we find a more complex reality.

Justice, biblically defined, is simply God's covenant faithfulness, God's integrity. It is God's unswerving commitment, first and foremost to himself, to his own honor and glory. But because of that self-commitment, it's also an unswerving dedication to keep the covenant that he has made with his people. In other words, God has staked his own reputation as a righteous God to the outcome of his covenant bond with us. That is to say, biblical justice or biblical righteousness is thoroughly grounded in the covenant and cannot be abstracted from the covenant. Justice and righteousness never operate outside of a covenantal framework in the Scripture. They're always qualified or defined by the covenant, which means that justice and righteousness are relational concepts. God gives to each his due regarding the covenant. God's justice is always good news to the faithful who are united to Christ. God's righteousness is not a synonym for his wrath, though it does include punishment for covenant breakers. The covenant has two sides: a blessing side for those who have faith and a cursing side for those who don't.

God's justice is often set in parallel with his covenant faithfulness. We have an example of this kind of parallelism[17] in Psalm 143: "Hear my prayer, O Lord, give ear to my supplications. In Your faithfulness answer me, and in Your righteousness." In the first pair of lines, "giving ear" is synonymous with "hear my prayer." In the next pair of lines, God's righteousness is defined in terms of his faithfulness. The Psalmist is appealing to God's righteousness: "Because you're righteous, hear my prayer. Because you're faithful, give ear to these things I'm bringing before you." Righteousness is synonymous with faithfulness, specifically faithfulness to the covenant.

God's obligation to us, then, does not come from outside, as if we had some intrinsic claim on God's salvation or as if our works could somehow put God in debt to us. Rather, God's obligation comes from within himself, from his own determination to be trustworthy and to make good on his freely made covenant pledge, no matter what. He gives us our due, so to speak, and repays us in accord with the provisions of the covenant bond. In Genesis 22, before God says anything about rewarding Abraham, he describes his own covenant oath. In the context, Abraham's obedience is not a form of merit but the proper response to the gracious covenant.

In the covenant of grace, God becomes a father and a husband to us and so he evaluates our works according to these relational categories. If my young son draws a family portrait of stick figures, I do not judge him for failing to measure up to the standards of Rembrandt or another one of the great artistic masters. Sure, I could give his drawing a devastating aesthetic critique. But because this is the work of my son, whom I love and accept, I hang the picture up on the refrigerator and when I look at it day after day after day, it makes me smile. If you saw the picture, it wouldn't have the same effect, because it was not

---

17   A Hebrew parallelism is when two lines in the Psalter are synonymous and are mutually interpreted.

drawn by your child. It doesn't do anything for you. You just see a stick figure. But I see something that has worth and value because of the father/son relationship.

Should I correct my son's picture and try to teach him to draw better? Yes, of course. And God does the same with us. God is easy to please but hard to satisfy. He can give us gentle reproofs and correctives, even as he rewards our efforts to do what is right.

We find another illustration of this in Jer. 10:24: "O Lord correct me but with justice; not in Your anger, lest You bring me to nothing." How many of us would ask God to correct us in his justice? "God, show me justice." But, again, we've got a wrong-headed idea of what justice is. It's not asking God to give us what we deserve in this absolute sense because then we'd all be in hell. Jeremiah makes his request within the context of the covenant relationship so that justice is understood as God's covenant righteousness. Within that covenant relationship, God will correct Jeremiah as a father.

In Daniel 9, the prophet is praying and confessing, not only for his own sin but for the sin of the people. In Dan. 9:16, right after listing all the transgressions of the people, he says, "O Lord, according to all Your righteousness, I pray, let Your anger and Your fury be turned away from Your city Jerusalem, Your holy mountain; because for our sins, and the iniquities of our fathers, Jerusalem and Your people are a reproach to all those around us." We would be far more inclined to say, "Lord, in your graciousness or in your mercy, turn your anger away from us." But Daniel prays "In your righteousness, turn your anger away from your people and away from their sins." What is Daniel doing? In praying that God would act in accord with his righteousness, he is pleading for mercy on the basis of God's promises. This is like a son coming to his father and saying, "Dad, remember, you promised that you would take me to the baseball game if I did my chores." A righteous dad will keep his promises; a smart son will appeal to the father's righteousness as a way of pleading the promises that have been made.

All these aspects of God's righteousness are packed into Ruth 2:12. When Boaz says to Ruth, "The Lord repay you for your good works," Boaz is not thinking like a Pelagian, he's thinking like a good covenant man. He's speaking like a good, faithful keeper of the covenant, who understands the father/child relationship, within which Ruth's good works will be evaluated and rewarded.

Pastorally, it is important to note that this opens a whole new avenue to assurance. We know that Scripture and the Westminster Confession teach that our good works are a means of assurance, but it is often hard for us to find assurance in our obedience because our works never seem to measure up. How good do our works have to be? How can we be assured we are God's people when our obedience is so imperfect? Understanding the covenant and the father/son dynamic that is at work is helpful to begin unpacking this biblical idea.

Appendix D

THE *GOEL* AND THE *LEVIR:* AN ANALYSIS
OF THE KINSMAN-REDEEMER

Some crucial themes will help unpack the rich theology of Ruth 3. Two significant issues are the *goel* and the *levirate*. The first is the Hebrew name for an Old Testament institution and the second is a Latin name for an Old Testament institution. The book of Ruth has a very intricate legal foundation, rooted deeply in Mosaic law. The story of Ruth interfaces with these two important legal institutions. In fact, Ruth 3 and Ruth 4 do not make a lot of sense apart from an understanding of these two institutions.

The *goel* is the Hebrew word for kinsman-redeemer; the *levirate* is a type of *goel*. The *goel* is the broader of these two concepts and includes or at least overlaps with the levirate, and so we will focus on that theme first. The *goel* is a critical figure in the Old Testament and points us to Jesus Christ.

One of the main purposes of the book of Ruth is to show the people of God their need for a *goel* and to foreshadow a coming kinsman-redeemer, Jesus Christ, the greater Boaz. What is a kinsman-redeemer? It is a relative (a kinsman) who redeems and rescues another family member in need. The institution presupposes covenantal bonds and solidarity between the one who is in need of redemption and the one who does the redeeming.

The redeemer acts on that bond to rescue, deliver, or to liberate his family member, usually at great cost to himself. Thus, the kinsman-redeemer shows *hesed,* the deep covenant loyalty that shows up several times in the book of Ruth.

The Responsibilities of a Kinsman-Redeemer

What were the potential responsibilities of a kinsman-redeemer? According to Lev. 25:48-49, a kinsman-redeemer was a close blood-relative. It could be a brother or an uncle or a cousin. Apparently, there would be some order as to who would take responsibility for the person in need or who was in trouble, beginning with the closest relative and moving out from there. A kinsman-redeemer would have to be wealthy enough to pay a ransom to rescue a poor, weak, helpless, or vulnerable relative. Or he would have to be strong enough to avenge the blood of his murdered relative.

A kinsman-redeemer had five primary duties. Let us look briefly at each one.

First, the kinsman-redeemer had to ransom a relative who sold himself into slavery. His first responsibility is liberation. We find this in Lev. 25:47:

> If a stranger or sojourner with you becomes rich, and your brother beside him becomes poor and sells himself to the stranger or sojourner with you or to a member of the stranger's clan...

So if an Israelite has to sell himself into slavery, the Israelite is undergoing the exodus in reverse. He's going back into a situation similar to the nation's slavery in Egypt. Thus, he needs a Moses-like figure who will be a kinsman-redeemer and rescue him out of that plight. This is how it is described in Lev. 25:48-55:

> ...then after he is sold he may be redeemed. One of his brothers may redeem him, for his uncle or his cousin may redeem him, or a close relative from his clan may redeem him.

Or if he grows rich he may redeem himself. He shall calculate with his buyer from the year when he sold himself to him until the year of jubilee, and the price of his sale shall vary with the number of years. The time he was with his owner shall be rated as the time of a hired worker. If there are still many years left, he shall pay proportionately for his redemption some of his sale price. If there remain but a few years until the year of jubilee, he shall calculate and pay for his redemption in proportion to his years of service. He shall treat him as a worker hired year by year. He shall not rule ruthlessly over him in your sight. And if he is not redeemed by these means, then he and his children with him shall be released in the year of jubilee. For it is to me that the people of Israel are servants. They are my servants whom I brought out of the land of Egypt: I am the LORD your God.

Here we discover the rationale for the kinsman-redeemer's responsibilities. God says the Israelites are *my* servants, so they're not to be enslaved to anyone else. If an Israelite is enslaved to a foreigner, his close relative has the responsibility to buy him out of that predicament. In doing so, the kinsman will be replicating the exodus, doing for his brother what God did for the nation when he brought them out of slavery in Egypt.

The second responsibility of the kinsman-redeemer is to avenge the name of an oppressed or murdered relative. That is, he must act as the blood avenger. We find these duties described in several places in the Old Testament law, particularly in Deut. 19:11-13:

But if anyone hates his neighbor, lies in wait for him, rises against him and strikes him mortally so that he dies then the elders of his city shall send and bring him from there, and deliver him over to the hand of the avenger of blood that he may die. Your eye shall not pity him, but you shall put away the guilt of innocent blood from Israel, that it may go well with you.

Essentially, the kinsman-redeemer will act as the avenger of blood and do against a Cain figure what no one was authorized to do in Genesis 4. Remember, the blood of Abel cried out from the ground. He was innocent and yet he was murdered by his brother. His blood cried out for vengeance. But there was no avenger of blood at that stage in history. Now the Israelites have been given this responsibility of being blood avengers, of executing judgment on the Cains in their midst.

It is crucial to understand that when the blood avenger goes to avenge the death of his relative, this is not a Hatfield and McCoy kind of blood feud. This is lawful vengeance, controlled and regulated by God's Word. Actually, it's very clear the *goel* is not taking the law into his own hands. This is not a vigilante system of revenge. It's clear the *goel* is acting as an agent of the state. That's why if the murderer flees to one of the cities of refuge, the elders are responsible to hand the murderer over. The official representatives, the governors of that city, hand the man over to be executed. The *goel*, in a sense, becomes an agent of the state's justice, and of course, also an agent of God's justice.

Num. 35:16-21 reads:

> But if he struck him down with an iron object, so that he died, he is a murderer. The murderer shall be put to death. And if he struck him down with a stone tool that could cause death, and he died, he is a murderer. The murderer shall be put to death. Or if he struck him down with a wooden tool that could cause death, and he died, he is a murderer. The murderer shall be put to death. The avenger of blood shall himself put the murderer to death; when he meets him, he shall put him to death. And if he pushed him out of hatred or hurled something at him, lying in wait, so that he died, or in enmity struck him down with his hand, so that he died, then he who struck the blow shall be put to death. He is a murderer. The avenger of blood shall put the murderer to death when he meets him.

The third responsibility is to regain a relative's forfeited inheritance. That is, to buy back their land for them. Remember, the land was typological; it pointed ahead to the kingdom of God and ultimately to the eschatological new creation. So, as an Israelite, maintaining your stake in the promised land was symbolic of your stake in the kingdom of God and participation in the kingdom of God. So it was important to not give up that inheritance. If you did have to forfeit that inheritance for some reason, the kinsman-redeemer would make sure it was returned to you. If a close relative has to give up his share of the promised land, it's the conquest in reverse. The land that was conquered and parcelled out under Joshua has been lost. The kinsman-redeemer re-enacts the conquest by regaining the lost land for the poor relative.

Fourth, the kinsman-redeemer had the role of defense attorney. The kinsman-redeemer was to see that justice was done in various situations. In the book of Job, Job cries out for a kinsman-redeemer who will act as a mediator who will go before God and plead his case. Job himself, of course, is a Christ figure. He's a suffering servant who ultimately overcomes and silences Satan. But Job also cries out for a Christ figure, a kinsman-redeemer who will come as a mediator between him and God, who will plead his case before God, and see to it that justice is done.

Then, fifthly, the kinsman-redeemer has the responsibility to play the role of a *levir*. The levirate law essentially said that the kinsman-redeemer would marry the wife of a widowed kinsman if he left no sons. As levirate, he would raise up a seed through the woman to carry on the deceased man's name and inheritance. This is the scenario we have in the book of Ruth: a man marries a woman, he dies without producing a male offspring who can carry on his name and maintain his inheritance, so there is need for a replacement husband.

Typically, the deceased man's brother would marry his widow, and through her, raise up a son to replace his deceased brother. That first son that he raises up through her will take the place of his deceased brother and her deceased husband and will carry on his name and inheritance. Of course, other children he has with her, now that she is his wife, will be his own children. But the first child becomes a replacement for his deceased brother. The structure of the *levirate* is essentially the Bible's two Adam theology. The Apostle Paul makes this plain in several places in his writings. If the first Adam dies without multiplying, without filling the earth, so to speak, then a second Adam is to come and carry out his tasks. That's just what we have with the *levirate*. The first Adam (the first husband) is fallen, so a second Adam (the kinsman-redeemer) comes to take his place. This is what we see played out in Ruth 3-4.

It should be obvious that when a man acted as a kinsman-redeemer, he was acting as a type of the Lord Jesus Christ. Christ is the one who ultimately performs these five duties on behalf of his people. In fact, in various places in the New Testament, we see Jesus explicitly presented as our kinsman-redeemer. Obviously, all the redemption language that is scattered throughout the New Testament points to Jesus as our *goel*. But there's one passage in particular that points to this institution. In Heb. 2:14-17, we read:

> Inasmuch then as the children have partaken of flesh and blood, He Himself likewise shared in the same, that through death He might destroy him who had the power of death, that is, the devil, and release those who through fear of death were all their lifetime subject to bondage. For indeed He does not give aid to angels, but He does give aid to the seed of Abraham. Therefore, in all things He had to be made like His brethren that he might be a merciful and faithful High Priest in things pertaining to God, to make propitiation for the sins of the people.

God became incarnate — he became our kinsman — in order to redeem us.

Hebrews 2 stresses that Jesus shares in the flesh of Abraham. He came to help the seed of Abraham. He's a kinsman-redeemer for the line of Abraham. We might then ask, "What good does that do for Gentiles who are not part of the family of Abraham?"

Paul shows us, especially in Romans, Galatians, and Ephesians that Gentiles are now being grafted into Israel and becoming part of the stock of the true Israel. We see this anticipated in the book of Ruth as Ruth herself is grafted into Israel and becomes a kind of honorary Israelite (cf. Romans 11).

The Kinsman-Redeemer Fulfilled in Jesus Christ

How has Christ redeemed us? How has he executed his responsibilities as a kinsman-redeemer? Christ has fulfilled each of the kinsman-redeemer's five responsibilities.

The first responsibility is that of liberating slaves. Christ has set the captives free. In Luke 4, Christ applies Isaiah 61 to himself. Isaiah 61 is one of the places where the prophet foretells of a kinsman-redeemer who will come to liberate his people. In the first Adam, all of us were made bondservants to sin, to Satan, to death, but Christ paid the ransom price and set us free. Jesus released us from these cruel taskmasters and purchased us, not with silver or gold, but with his own priceless blood. Moses was a kinsman-redeemer who freed his enslaved brethren. Jesus is the greater Moses performing a greater exodus to free us as slaves.

Secondly, what about being a blood avenger? Christ avenges us against our enemies. This is why Rom. 12:19 forbids Christians to take vengeance into their own hands. We don't avenge ourselves; we give way and let Christ take vengeance for us. And he certainly will. Sometimes this is accomplished through the state as Christ's agent, which is what Paul describes in Romans 13. But more than that, we can say that through Christ's judgment at the end of history, he will avenge the blood of his persecuted people. In the book of Revelation, the martyred saints cry out, "How long till we are avenged?" And Christ answers this plea by the end of the book. Of course, we can say the ultimate slayer of God's people is Satan himself. Christ has utterly destroyed him and triumphed over him at the cross. John 8 tells us that Satan was a murderer from the beginning, but Christ has defeated him.

The third responsibility of the kinsman-redeemer is winning back a lost inheritance. Christ has regained our forfeited inheritance. Because of the sin of the first Adam, we've all been exiled from our home. When Adam sinned, we sinned. When Adam was exiled from the Garden of Eden, we were exiled from the Garden of Eden. We've all been exiled from our home; we've all been expelled from the kingdom; we've all forfeited our inheritance in the paradise of God. We lost our title deed to the earth in the first Adam, but Jesus Christ, as our kinsman-redeemer, restores our inheritance to us. In Christ, the earth becomes ours once again. This is why Paul can say to the church at Corinth, "All things belong to you." Our inheritance has been won back for us in and through Christ Jesus.

We can say this is not only true in the world to come, in the resurrection, but it's true in principle even now. As the gospel spreads, as the knowledge of God fills the earth, God's people claim their inheritance in Christ.

Fourth, Christ acts as our *goel* in that he is our legal defender. Christ is an advocate for his people. In 1 John 1:8-10, we read:

> If we say we have no sin, we deceive ourselves, and the truth is not in us. If we confess our sins, he is faithful and just to forgive us our sins and to cleanse us from all unrighteousness. If we say we have not sinned, we make him a liar, and his word is not in us.

Why is it comforting to know that Jesus is defending us in the great tribunal of God's court? Because his blood was shed to make propitiation for our sins. Propitiation means he has turned aside the wrath of God. He pleads our cause before the Father. He defends us against the accusations of Satan, and, of course, his pleas to the Father always prevail because of what he has done for us. We will never hear, "Guilty as charged," because a justifying verdict over our lives has been secured by Christ.

Fifth, the kinsman-redeemer would marry the widowed kin and raise up seed. When the first Adam died, he left his bride barren. He failed to bring a seed of promise into the world. So there's a need for a second Adam, a second husband, to come and marry the widow and through her to raise up a seed who will reclaim the inheritance. Isa. 53:4-8 describes the Lord performing this duty for his people. It is ultimately, of course, fulfilled in Christ. He is the one through whom the barren widow produces offspring, as the prophet foretold.

It's important to understand how the work of the *goel* in Old Testament law reflects Yahweh's own saving work for Israel, which ultimately comes to fulfillment in Jesus Christ. Isaiah 40-66 comes back to this whole notion of God as deliverer and redeemer again and again. All the responsibilities of the *goel* are found in Isaiah. Yahweh is going to fulfill these responsibilities on behalf of his people. Isaiah addresses the nation in the context of exile and enslavement, and through the prophet, the Lord promises a new exodus and a new conquest.

It should be obvious from all this that the kinsman-redeemer provides a comprehensive salvation. He redeems your property, your person, and your posterity. There's nothing left unredeemed by the kinsman-redeemer. Christ, as our kinsman-redeemer has secured our inheritance of eternal life, defeated our enemies, and raised up innumerable seed to populate his kingdom. The kinsman-redeemer in the Old Covenant was acting out in advance what Christ would do on our behalf.

There are three kinsman-redeemer figures in the book of Ruth. There is the unnamed man in Ruth 4 who fails to perform his duties. He was willing to redeem the land, but then he backed off when he discovered that he would have to marry Ruth and raise up seed. He is a false kinsman-redeemer, like the first Adam. When he realizes there are going to be personal costs, he doesn't want to pay them. Then there's Obed, who is the child born to Boaz and Ruth. He's called a kinsman-redeemer at the end of the book because he is the one who will replace Elimelech and his two sons. The whole kinsman-redeemer theme is concludes with Obed because he is the one who will replace all the deceased men and carry on the family name. The third kinsman-redeemer in the book is, of course, Boaz, who is the central kinsman-redeemer figure in the book of Ruth. He is the one who performs two major *goel* duties in this book. He regains a lost inheritance and raises up an heir to preserve Elimelech's line.

THE LEVIRATE LAW

Now let's turn to a more specific discussion of the *levirate* law. The first point to make is to say that the levirate institution has nothing directly to do with Levi or with the Levites. The word "levirate" comes from a Latin word which means "husband's brother." As we have already seen, the *levirate* duty is just one of the responsibilities that a *goel* must perform. The basic law here is found in Deut. 25:5-10:

> If brothers dwell together, and one of them dies and has no son, the wife of the dead man shall not be married outside the family to a stranger. Her husband's brother shall go in to her and take her as his wife and perform the duty of a husband's brother to her. And the first son whom she bears shall succeed to the name of his dead brother, that his name may not be blotted out of Israel. And if the man does not wish to take his brother's wife, then his brother's wife shall go up to the gate to the elders and say, "My husband's brother refuses to perpetuate his brother's name in Israel; he will not perform the duty of a husband's brother to me." Then the elders of his city shall call him and speak to him, and if he persists, saying, "I do not wish to take her," then his brother's wife shall go up to him in the presence of the elders and pull his sandal off his foot and spit in his face. And she shall answer and say, "So shall it be done to the man who does not build up his brother's house." And the name of his house shall be called in Israel, "The house of him who had his sandal pulled off."

The idea behind this law is not as complicated as it sounds: When a wife's husband died, leaving her sonless, without a male heir, his brother would marry her, and the first child born of that union would take the name and inheritance of the deceased man.

The man who performed the duty of the levir did so at great cost to himself. It was a sacrificial act of love, as he built up his brother's house at his own expense.

This law shows up in the New Testament in Mark 12:18ff where the Sadducees use it in an attempt to trick Jesus. They try to play off the doctrine of the levirate institution against a bodily resurrection. They describe a situation in which a woman goes through a series of husbands who keep dying. Each successive *levir* perishes, making her a widow again. The Sadducees then ask whose wife she will be in the resurrection. Of course, Jesus goes on to explain they have misunderstood the nature of resurrection life.

There are a lot of twists and turns in the book of Ruth that make use of the *levirate* institution complex. Before we get into that, several practical questions come up in discussion of this law. First, Deut. 25:5 makes it clear the law only applies to brothers (or close relatives) who are living together, which probably indicates that it was only a responsibility for those who were roughly the same age. It would not be hard to imagine situations where the law would have been virtually impossible to carry out. For example, say that a man who is married dies without producing offspring and his younger brother was, say, two years old. Does she have to wait around until he's old enough to marry? If she had to wait, it might result in her marrying at an age when she could no longer bear a child, which would defeat the purpose of the law.

Given that the obligation applies to brothers who live together, it also suggests there was some kind of family approval needed for a marriage. If you are a younger brother and your older brother is getting married you may consider at least once that if he dies without raising up a male child, she would become your wife. So, the fact that they're living together probably indicates the brothers might have some influence in their older brother's choice of a wife. That is, they might have some say in the matter, or at least the older brother's choice of a particular young woman would need wider family approval.

Also, since the brothers must live together, it's likely that none of the other brothers are married. This is another question that comes up. What if a man is married and he dies without producing a male child and all his other brothers are married? Does one of them have to take her on as a second wife? Does this set up a kind of legitimate polygamous situation? Commentators actually debate this question. Some say it must have validated a polygamous scenario. But that seems very unlikely. The idea of brothers living together indicates that it is brothers who are not yet married, so polygamy was not required or expected. After all, while we see polygamy sometimes being practiced in the Old Testament, there is no question it was considered a violation of God's law. Polygamy is contrary to the creation ordinance of marriage set up in Genesis 1-2. We shouldn't think the *levirate* law required God's people to do things that were completely impractical or contrary to other divine laws.

Some have also wondered: Did a *levirate* union produce a real, permanent marriage? Or only a temporary marriage for the sake of raising up a son in the place of the deceased? Given the high view of marriage found everywhere in Scripture, a temporary sexual arrangement is hard to imagine. Most likely, *levirate* marriages were real marriages.

What happens to the man who refuses to perform his *levirate* duty? Deuteronomy 25 implies he will be publicly humiliated for refusing to carry on his brother's name. By refusing to carry on his brother's name, he is given a name of shame. Deut. 25:10 reads: "His name shall be called the House of Him Who Had His Sandal Removed." He is ashamed in two ways: First, his sandal is pulled off his foot, and then secondly, his face is spat upon.

There's a kind of *lex talonis* at work there. Instead of eye for eye, tooth for tooth, the principle at work in the levirate law is name for name. He refused to build up his brother's name, and so his own name is torn down. He refused to build up his brother's house, and so his house is going to be torn down.

What does it mean that his face is spat upon? This does not happen in Ruth, but the meaning is obvious. Spitting in the face is an obvious sign of disrespect. Think of those who spat upon Jesus when he was being crucified. They were seeking to show he was not the true kinsman-redeemer, that he could not be a new Adam taking the place of the fallen Adam. Of course, they were wrong.

What about the custom described in Deuteronomy 25 of a man having his sandal removed? Scripture uses the feet as a euphemism for the private parts. (This may be happening in Ruth 3.) Thus, it could be that removing the sandal is a symbolic way of exposing this man's private parts. To remove the sandal from the foot — if feet are understood euphemistically as a symbol of the private parts — would be like disrobing the man. It would be a form of public humiliation, at least symbolically. To take off his sandal would be like pulling his pants down in public and saying this man can't do what he's been called to do, so he isn't a true man.

There could also be a reference here to his refusal to stand in his own shoes and take responsibility for his actions, the way that Adam does in Genesis 3. In Genesis, Adam won't assume responsibility for what he does. He refuses to stand in his own shoes, so to speak, and assume the responsibility for his actions.

In the book of Ruth, when Boaz transacts with this closer relative to see who's going to perform the levirate duty with Ruth, they actually exchange sandals, which is a little bit different from what is described in Deuteronomy 25. But clearly they are exchanging roles and responsibilities, so it seems to be an application of the law to that particular situation. There is still shame involved, however, noted most clearly in the text by the fact that the man who won't perform the levirate responsibility with Ruth is not named. It just speaks of him as a man, but it never gives his name. He has no name because he won't carry on the name of his deceased brother.His name is lost whereas Boaz' name is made great.

The Vindication of Tamar

Genesis 38 is one of those chapters in Scripture that's very troubling. In the midst of the story about Joseph's great faithfulness, we find this story thrown in about Judah's unfaithfulness in Canaan. Joseph is down in Egypt living faithfully; Judah is up in Canaan in the land of promise living unfaithfully. That's the contrast being made in the text. Judah is forfeiting his standing and place in the family as the royal son, and in some way Joseph is taking his place (though Judah will eventually be redeemed and restored.). Since Genesis 38 deals with the tribe of Judah and with the *levirate*, it's critical for our understanding of Ruth.

By the time we get to Genesis 38, we know Judah is the chosen tribe. The first three sons have already disqualified themselves, in Genesis 34 through Genesis 35, and so now the focus is on Judah. What will Judah do? Will he be a faithful man and prove himself worthy of being the royal leader, the tribe from which the king will come? In Genesis 38, Judah marries outside the covenant line, just like the Sethites in Genesis 6, instead of following the example of Isaac and Jacob. Judah has a son named Ur who marries Tamar, but Ur dies without leaving Tamar a son. Thus the *levirate* institution kicks in (obviously it was a pre-Mosaic institution).

Ur died without producing a son. His younger brother Onan has to perform the duty of a levir. Onan pretends to be a *levir*, but each time he sleeps with Tamar he lets his seed fall on the ground. (Contrary to some readings of the story, he is not killed for practicing a form of birth control, per se, but for violating the *levirate* duty.) Now, why does he want to do this? It's because he is self-seeking. He doesn't want to build up his brother's house. He wants to, in fact, steal his brother's inheritance. If he has a son, that son would take Ur's place and would receive the inheritance of the firstborn. But if Tamar does not have a son, Onan would become the firstborn, because his older brother is dead, and so he would get a double share. He needs to make sure Tamar has no children.

But he can't just say that he doesn't want to be a *levir* because then Tamar would be passed on to the next brother and she could still have a son through him. So this is Onan's dilemma: on the one hand, he can't just turn down the *levirate* responsibilities without passing Tamar to the next brother but he does not want to raise up a son through Tamar. Onan's solution is to sleep with her but avoid getting her pregnant. Of course, God sees his wickedness and kills him.

So it falls to Judah's son Shelah to perform the duty of a *levirate* marriage. At this point in the story, Judah is acting very wickedly. He doesn't see that his two sons died because they displeased the Lord. Instead, he starts to think there must be something wrong with Tamar. If God keeps killing her husbands, obviously she's in sin. She must be bad luck. Judah makes false promises to Tamar. He says he is going to give her Shelah, but he doesn't intend to do so. He keeps holding things off, delaying the marriage. When Shelah is fully grown, Tamar realizes the marriage is not going to come to pass. Tamar knows at this point that Judah is the chosen tribe and that the promised seed will come through Judah's line. She knows there must be a seed of Judah. So she takes matters into her own hands and acts in a clever, deceptive way to ensure there is an heir. She dresses up like a harlot and tricks Judah into playing the *levir* himself by sleeping with him. She gives birth to Judah's son and then proves it to him.

It's easy to critique Tamar for what she does here. But we need to be careful. The story itself does not condemn Tamar for her actions. Tamar acted in this manner because she had concern for the seed line. She was probably just as disgusted by what she was doing as we are when we read the story. She did not do this out of any sense of passionate love for Judah or out of unbridled lust. She only does what she does because she has concern for the covenant and for producing a son who will carry on the promised seed line.

Readers need to be careful about reading these stories in a moralistic sense; we've got to read them theologically. When we do that, we see that what Tamar does in Genesis 38 is not all that different from what Ruth is going to do in Ruth 3. It's clear in the book of Ruth that her actions vindicate her. When she crawls into bed with Boaz and says, essentially, "Be a *goel* and a *levirate* for me," she's doing the same thing that Tamar did with Judah, but without the deception.

It is clear that Tamar and Ruth act righteously in pursuing a *levir*. The point of these stories is not to make either woman a moral example to imitate (especially since the *levirate* institution has expired). Instead, we have to look at it theologically and ask how these actions fit into God's redemptive design. What concerns each woman is raising up a seed to take the place of the deceased, of seeing to it that the covenant line continues. Ruth and Tamar are not showing women how to get husbands any more than Abraham shows us how to parent in Genesis 22 when he takes Isaac up on the mountain and is ready to stab him to death.

Tamar, Ruth, and Abraham are viewed as righteous, even though their actions do not fit neatly with any code of ethics. In Tamar's case, in Gen. 38:26, Judah acknowledges the righteousness of Tamar's action. When it is revealed that Judah did not sleep with a prostitute but slept with his daughter-in-law, to whom he should have provided a son as a husband, he realizes he had been trapped in his sin. He realizes what Tamar has done, and he says she is more righteous than him. He vindicates her and condemns himself for his action. He was tricked by her into doing the right thing.

In Ruth 4:12, the community holds up Tamar as an ideal matriarch. She's compared to Ruth. She is a model for Ruth; a model of virtue because of her love for the covenant and her desire to honor the covenant. Like Ruth and Rahab, Tamar is one of the righteous Gentile women who is included and singled out for inclusion in the genealogy of Jesus Christ in the gospel of Matthew. Everything seems to point to her vindication. Ruth and Tamar are both women who are "saved in childbearing" (1 Tim. 2:15).

There's certainly a lot more that could be said about Genesis 38, but for our purposes, it's enough to see that failure to perform the *levirate* duty is what gets Judah in trouble. Judah would not fulfill the *levirate* responsibility and failed to provide his sons for Tamar, manifesting his unfaithfulness. Perez, the son, born to Tamar out of wedlock, is a sign of her righteousness and his shame because of Judah's sin.

<hr />

THE CASE FOR DAVIDIC KINGSHIP

Now, according to Deut. 23:2, a child of illegitimate birth, born out of wedlock (like Perez), was excluded from holding office in the commonwealth of Israel. In Gen. 49:10, Judah is promised to be the tribe from which the messianic king will come. There's a sense in which that promise in Gen. 49:10 had to be full of bitter irony for Judah since he had already disqualified his descendants from any rule for generations to come. But this is where the story of Ruth comes in.

Just as a failure to perform the *levirate* duty got Judah into trouble and disqualified the tribe of Judah from the kingship, so it's the performance of the *levirate* by another Judahite, Boaz, that preserves Judah's royal line and ultimately produces the king who fulfilled the promise of Genesis 49. Of course, this is David. For this reason, the book of Ruth ends with a genealogy. Judah disqualified his line from any royal office in Israel to the tenth generation (Deut. 23:2) because he slept with Tamar out of wedlock.

But if we count the generations in the genealogy of Ruth 4, we find the tenth generation is David. This is the first generation of Judah's line that would have been eligible to hold royal office in Israel. Boaz' *levirate* marriage undoes the damage of Judah's refusal to be a true *levir* and produces a royal son. Boaz is what Judah should have been. And David is the ultimate man of Judah, the lion of the tribe of Judah.

There is a profound beauty in what God does: Just as Judah falls into sin by failing to perform the *levirate,* so when Boaz comes along and performs the *levirate,* the tribe of Judah is restored. And, of course, ultimately Jesus Christ's lineage is traced back through this genealogy in Ruth 4.

The levirate is the hinge on which the whole story of Ruth turns. To get what's going on in Ruth, we must connect it with Deuteronomy 25 and Genesis 38. Ruth reverses the curse on Judah from Genesis 38 and shows us the full restoration of Judah. The book provides legitimate grounds for the kingship of David and, of course, for the kingship of David's greater son, Jesus Christ.

CPSIA information can be obtained
at www.ICGtesting.com
Printed in the USA
LVHW021409280421
685859LV00025B/289